TIMEF

HORSES TO FOLLOW

2019 FLAT SEASON

CONTENTS

TIMEF0RM

ISBN 978-1-9997783-4-7   Price £9.95

Printed and bound by
Charlesworth Press,
Wakefield, UK 01924 204830

SECTION

Timeform's Fifty To Follow, carefully chosen by members of Timeform's editorial staff, are listed below with their respective page numbers. A selection of ten (**marked in bold with a ★**) is made for those who prefer a smaller list.

The form summary for each horse is shown after its age, colour, sex and pedigree. The summary shows the distance, the state of the going and where the horse finished in each of its races on the Flat during 2018. Performances are in chronological sequence with the date of its last race shown at the end.

The distance of each race is given in furlongs, fractional distances being expressed in the decimal notation to the nearest tenth of a furlong. Races run in Britain on all-weather surfaces are prefixed by 'f' for fibresand, 'p' for polytrack and 't' for tapeta. The going is symbolised as follows: f=firm (turf) or fast (all-weather), m=good to firm (turf) or standard to fast (all-weather); g=good (turf) or standard (all-weather), d=good to soft/dead (turf) or standard to slow (all-weather); s=soft (turf) or slow (all-weather); v=heavy.

Placings are indicated, up to the sixth place, by use of superior figures, an asterisk being used to denote a win.

The Timeform Rating of a horse is simply the merit of the horse expressed in pounds and is arrived at by careful examination of its running against other horses. The ratings range from 130+ for tip-top performers down to a figure of around 20 for the poorest. Symbols attached to the ratings: 'p'–likely to improve; 'P'–capable of much better form; '+'–the horse may be better than we have rated it.

Bangkok (Ire) 91p

3 b.c. Australia – Tanaghum (Darshaan)
2018 7m² 7m⁴ 8m⁴ Sep 27

Whether the now well-established colours of King Power Racing will be as prominent on British racecourses in years to come remains to be seen, with Vichai Srivaddhanaprabha having passed away so tragically last October. Looking to the more immediate future, though, and there is no shortage of interesting prospects set to race in the Thai businessman's memory in 2019, not least Andrew Balding's Bangkok, who has the potential to be one of the operation's leading lights this term.

Bought for 500,000 guineas as a yearling, this leggy, athletic individual immediately marked himself down as a potential Group horse when second on his debut in a seven-furlong novice event at Newmarket in July. In a race dominated by the progeny of a couple of highly-promising first-crop sires, Bangkok travelled strongly and powered to the front over a furlong out, before being gradually worn down (beaten a neck, with six lengths back to the remainder) by the imposing Sangarius, a beautifully-bred Kingman colt who made a successful transition to listed company next time before running with credit in the Dewhurst.

Bangkok is best judged on that initial effort for now, as things didn't exactly go to plan subsequently. Having disappointed at Ascot in September, he then wasn't seen to best effect when fourth in a race that has already thrown up no less than six subsequent winners back at Newmarket (Rowley) later that month; he was forced to deliver his challenge wider and from further back than the other principals (all drawn high), ultimately doing well under the circumstances to be beaten only four and a quarter lengths.

Raced up to a mile so far, everything in Bangkok's pedigree points to him excelling over longer trips. He's by English and Irish Derby winner Australia and related to several who enjoyed success over middle-distances, including the smart Tactic, so expect ongoing improvement as his stamina is drawn out in 2019. A novice is a formality and a mark of 88 surely underestimates him but, beyond that, he can hold his own in pattern company. **Andrew Balding**

Conclusion: *Showed fairly useful form at two and should have more to offer when granted the opportunity to tackle middle-distances*

Baritone (Ire)   94p

4 b.g. Camelot – Star Ruby (Ire) (Rock of Gibraltar (Ire))
2018 10v² 10.3g⁴ 10m³ 11.2m³ 12v* 12m Oct 12

A horse who has already raced seven times and been successful only once—in a weak three-runner Pontefract maiden at that—wouldn't be an obvious candidate for selection in this publication, but we're going to let you in on a little secret: Baritone was one of the very first names on the list. It's not what he's done already that sets him apart from the crowd, but what we think he'll go on to achieve in 2019, a thought underpinned by a distinct air of untapped potential.

Baritone started his career in the autumn of his juvenile season, finishing a promising fifth in a Newbury maiden, and his six starts in 2018 were spread out from April to October, highlighting the patient approach of his handler Sir Michael Stoute that so often pays dividend in a horse's fourth year. Bartione's maiden win may have come relatively late in the season, but it was his three previous runs that pegged him as one to follow. A good fourth in a Chester maiden in May—just behind another member of this year's *Fifty*, Infrastructure, and the now smart Argentello—he then shaped encouragingly when third on his handicap debut at Ascot in July, finishing hot on the heels of a pair of promising individuals in Elwazir and Extra Elusive. Add to that an encouraging run at Goodwood, when finishing well from a long way back to snatch third (having also been forced just about widest of all), and you have the recipe for a horse that is ready to take off. Baritone didn't show what he could do on his final start in the Old Rowley Cup at Newmarket (too free having been rushed up after a slow start), but he remains one to be very positive about for the year ahead; he remains lightly-raced over a mile and a half and is likely to stay further still. **Sir Michael Stoute**

Conclusion: *Improved with racing last season, bar a blip on his final start at Newmarket, and remains potentially well treated from a BHA mark of 85, with further progress on the cards*

Baryshnikov   85p

3 ch.g. Mastercraftsman (Ire) – Tara Moon (Pivotal)
2018 8g⁴ 8d³ p8g² Nov 17

There's a rich history of horses named after figures from the world of ballet. Triple Crown-winner Nijinsky is the first to spring to mind, but Oaks and Irish Derby heroine Balanchine (named after perhaps the most influential choreographer of the twentieth century) and the disqualified 1980 2,000 Guineas 'winner' Nureyev are other memorable ones. Baryshnikov, who like Nijinsky and Nureyev, is named after one of the greatest male ballet dancers in history, won't be emulating those classic winners in 2019, but he's one to follow at a rather less exalted level.

Baryshnikov ended 2018 a maiden after three runs, but he reached a fairly useful standard on the last two, when third and second in well-contested races at Newbury and Lingfield, respectively, chasing home subsequent listed winner Barys on the latter occasion. On the bare form of those efforts, he's done well to get into handicaps off a mark of 78, and the improvement that will surely be forthcoming when he steps up in trip—he's a son of Mastercraftsman and looks to be crying out for at least a mile and a quarter—ought to see him win a few races before the assessor is able to catch up. **Ed Walker**

Conclusion: *Starts out from a lenient-looking mark and likely to progress once upped in trip, making him a very interesting prospect for middle-distance handicaps*

Berkshire Blue (Ire) ★   107p

4 b.g. Champs Elysees – Lemon Rock (Green Desert (USA))
2018 11.2m⁴ t12.2s* 13g 12m* 13.9m⁵ Aug 25

York's Melrose Stakes—sometimes known as the three-year-old Ebor—is year in, year out one of the best handicaps of its type and a rich source of horses to follow. Last year's renewal had an especially deep look to it—Ghostwatch (winner), Proschema (third), Mekong (fourth), Corgi (sixth) and Blue Laureate (seventh) are all well worth looking out for in 2019—but it's the fifth-placed Berkshire Blue who makes the cut for the *Fifty*.

Unraced until June 2018, Berkshire Blue made rapid strides, confirming his debut promise when winning by 11 lengths at Wolverhampton in July. A Group 3 at Newmarket proved too much too soon on his next outing, but he was soon back on the up when defying a wide trip under 'Magic Man' Joao Moreira in a mile and a half handicap at the Shergar Cup. Subsequently raised to a mark of 95, Berkshire Blue was always in the firing line in the Melrose on his final start and went down fighting, beaten under two lengths in a well-run race in which the first eight finished clear. He's gone up another 3 lb since, but that's no issue judged on the York form—the winner and fourth fought out the finish of a listed race in the autumn—and Berkshire Blue has plenty of scope for further improvement after five starts in less than three months, his good-bodied physique another thing to recommend him. Berkshire Blue stays a mile and three quarters and acts on good to firm going and tapeta (he's unraced on going softer than good). He's in excellent hands to fulfil his potential. *Andrew Balding*

Conclusion: *Progressed well in a light three-year-old campaign and looks the type to go on improving in 2019, with the top middle-distance/staying handicaps likely to be on his agenda*

Blackheath   96

4 b.g. Excelebration (Ire) – Da's Wish (Ire) (Sadler's Wells (USA))
2018 t7.2g* p8s³ 7m⁶ 6f* 6.1m p6g² p6g⁴ 6g² Oct 3

Blackheath was a profitable member of last year's *Fifty*, winning twice from eight starts (at 4/1 and 11/2), but we were left with the feeling that it could—and probably should—have been more. With that in mind, we're more than happy to make him the sole holdover from the class of 2018.

Admittedly, Blackheath's problems were occasionally self-inflicted, a tendency to start slowly costing him once or twice. Hopefully that trait will be ironed out, but, in any case, there's plenty in the formbook to suggest that he's a well-treated sprinter with the potential for better yet. His handicap win at Salisbury last July worked out well and none of his four subsequent outings got to the bottom of him, but he still made the frame in three of them and again the form stacks up, notably his second to Encrypted (who went on to win a listed race) at Chelmsford. Back at Salisbury for his final start in October, Blackheath again found one too good, but he gave the winner Beyond Equal (who was winning his fourth handicap of the year and is himself one to note for 2019) a head start and was still closing at the line. A 2 lb rise to a mark of 84 leaves him still ahead of the handicapper on the strength of that form, and that's without accounting for the scope he has for further progress.

Blackheath has won over seven furlongs but is a strong traveller and seems at his best at six furlongs. He's effective on polytrack, tapeta and firm going (unraced on softer than good) and has a style of racing that suggests he should thrive in a big-field handicap. *Ed Walker*

Conclusion: *Strong-traveller who did well last season without ever really seeming to be bottomed out; has the potential to progress to the level needed for some of the best sprint handicaps*

Craster (Ire) 88p

3 b.c. Sea The Stars (Ire) – Coquet (Sir Percy)
2018 8s⁴ 10.2m³ 8d⁵ Oct 26

"I will be disappointed if she doesn't stay a mile and a quarter or a mile and a half, so we can dream about the Oaks."

Coquet had just won the Height of Fashion Stakes back in 2012, and her trainer Hughie Morrison—a man hardly predisposed to misplaced confidence—was quick to focus on the potential staying power of a filly who, little over a week later, finished a meritorious sixth (beaten under six lengths after meeting trouble in-running) behind Was in the big one at Epsom. At that time, it was long odds-on that Coquet would enjoy plenty more days in the sun, yet Goodwood would prove to be her third and final success in a career that ended in disappointing fashion, when she beat only one home—some sixty lengths behind the winner—in the Park Hill Stakes at Doncaster the following year.

Craster, Coquet's second foal after the fairly useful Glencadam Master, ended his first year winless, but, overall, the portents of that light introductory season suggest that the youngster can go a long way to mirroring his dam's progress when the emphasis is more on stamina. His second at Bath in October, when he went like a better animal than even the now-90 rated winner Themaxwecan, was his most striking performance as a two-year-old, though his two starts either side weren't without promise themselves; he was very green at Ffos Las on debut, and his fifth at Newbury could easily have been down to the drop in trip and return to softer ground.

Craster will return a different proposition over middle-distances in 2019, which may mean Morrison has cause to recycle the sort of bullish sentiments he unfurled on Coquet all those summers ago. ***Hughie Morrison***

Conclusion: *Likely to emulate the many positive aspects of his dam by developing into a very useful middle-distance performer, following a solid grounding in a brief juvenile campaign*

Crystal King 95p

4 ch.g. Frankel – Crystal Star (Mark of Esteem (Ire))
2018 11d 10m⁶ 11.2m⁶ p12d 10d* Oct 16

Sometimes when you look at something on paper it is difficult to envisage how it can fail. Take the golfer Adam Scott for example; ask any golf fan to name the best swings on Tour and it's odds-on that Scott's name would be amongst the first three mentioned. To be successful you obviously need more than just the right attributes on paper, and Scott is rightly heralded as one of the great underachievers of the game, but it's very easy to forget that he has 29 professional wins under his belt, including a Major, and spent a total of 11 weeks as world number one.

In terms of Adam Scott's equine equivalent, we need look no further than Crystal King. By Frankel and out of Crystal Star, the mare who has produced the high-class Crystal Ocean as well as the smart performers Hillstar, Crystal Zvezda and Crystal Capella, Crystal King's claims on paper are obvious but, unlike his relations, he has been something of a slow learner. He proved immature throughout his stint in maidens, and the signs were quite worrying when he also disappointed as a well-backed joint-favourite on his handicap debut, sweating up badly beforehand—albeit during one of the hottest Julys since 1910—and seemingly not in any fit state to do himself justice (finished well held). Connections clearly saw something in him, though, and freshened up by a 12-week break (during which time he was also gelded), Crystal King left a hint of what he may yet achieve when getting off the mark at Leicester, still showing his inexperience and taking a bit of stoking up but hitting his stride well late on to run out a convincing winner. The impression is that we've barely scratched the surface of Crystal King's ability and he is expected to end the season rated considerably higher than he starts it. *Sir Michael Stoute*

Conclusion: *Produced a career best to belatedly get off the mark on his final start and looks just the sort to flourish as a four-year-old given his pedigree and connections*

Dalaalaat (Ire)   81p
3 b.c. Kingman – Gile Na Greine (Ire) (Galileo (Ire))
2018 8d⁵ 8.3d* Oct 31

It might seem a strange thing to say about a horse who won seven of his eight starts and ended his career with a Group 1 four-timer, but we probably never saw the full extent of Kingman's ability. His Timeform rating of 134 puts him in exalted company, but the way that he quickened to win steadily-run races at Ascot, Goodwood and Deauville on his final three runs suggests he'd have given the 140 barrier a scare under the right circumstances. Alas, we never got to see him as a four-year-old, but racing's loss was breeding's gain judging by Kingman's first two-year-olds in 2018. Among his 24 individual winners worldwide were stakes winners Calyx, Persian King and Sangarius, but there were bundles of promising performers at a lower level, too, and we expect big things in 2019.

In terms of bare form, Dalaalaat was one of the lesser achievers among his sire's winners, but that's partly because his second-time-out win over a mile at Nottingham in October came in a steadily-run maiden that wasn't conducive to a big performance. His quality was nevertheless obvious to see—James Doyle just nudged him ahead late on—and he strongly appeals as the type to go on improving for a stable with few peers when it comes to maximising potential. Both of Dalaalaat's starts to date have been over a mile, a trip over which his sire and 117-rated dam did most of their racing, and there's unlikely to be any hurry to get him up in trip, though a mile and a quarter will almost certainly be within range when the times comes. **William Haggas**

Conclusion: *Well-connected type who wasn't all out to win his maiden and looks sure to climb through the handicap ranks in 2019*

Dancing Vega (Ire) ★   99P

3 ch.f. Lope de Vega (Ire) – We Can Say It Now (AUS) (Starcraft (NZ))
2018 8g* Oct 26

The Spanish Golden Age, which spanned much of the sixteenth century and stretched into the seventeenth, saw the likes of El Greco, Diego Velasquez, Cervantes and Félix Lope de Vega y Carpio come to artistic and literary prominence. One can only assume that the people behind the Waverley Racing operation appreciated the works of the last-named—more commonly known by his shortened name Lope de Vega—given that all four horses who carried their colours in 2018 were sired by the equine namesake of the prolific dramatist. Not only that, all were two-year-old fillies trained

Ralph Beckett has assembled a strong team of three-year-old fillies

by Ralph Beckett who, but for Antonia de Vega's effective no-show in the Fillies' Mile at Newmarket in October (she was subsequently found to be lame), would have gone through their first season of racing with unblemished records.

The merits of Feliciana de Vega's inclusion in our *Fifty* can be found later in this publication, and it wasn't a difficult decision to 'double up' such was the impression created by Dancing Vega when making a winning debut at Doncaster in October. Slowly into stride but soon handy, Dancing Vega simply toyed with her nine opponents, tanking along before eventually hitting the front over a furlong out, quickening clear thereafter in most impressive fashion, the 'large P' an indication that there is scope for significant improvement. Dancing Vega was immediately given quotes of between 25/1 and 33/1 for both the 1000 Guineas and Oaks, and the form was given a boost just eight days later, when the runner-up Blue Gardenia went one better in the listed Montrose Stakes on the Rowley Mile.

Dancing Vega's dam was a Group 1-winner at a mile in New Zealand, and given her half-brother Sky Kingdom and half-sister Tranquil Star both tasted success at around a mile and a quarter, there's a chance that Dancing Vega's ideal trip may fall between that of the two British fillies' classics. One thing is for sure; whichever route Dancing Vega takes in 2019, we are keen to keep her on side. ***Ralph Beckett***

Conclusion: *Created a deep impression when making a winning debut in a back end maiden at Doncaster and has the potential to develop into one of the best of her generation*

David Johnson, Flat Horse Racing Editor (Dancing Vega): *"Ralph Beckett and Waverley Racing hardly look short of talent among their three-year-old fillies for 2019, and I'm hopeful that Dancing Vega will prove the pick of them—in fact, she could easily make into one of the best of her sex. She did all she could on her only juvenile start in impressive fashion and the form received a big boost with the runner up winning in listed company on her next start. Whether it proves to be the Guineas or the Oaks, Dancing Vega has genuine classic potential."*

Dazzling Dan (Ire)   99
3 b.g. Dandy Man (Ire) – Scrumptious (Sakhee (USA))
2018 6.1g⁴ 6m² 6d² 6d* Nov 10

It makes this writer feel rather old, and perhaps some readers will feel the same, to learn that it's getting on for 13 years since Speciosa provided trainer Pam Sly with a fairy-tale win in the 1,000 Guineas. It's long odds against that such a dizzying high will ever be repeated, and mid-grade handicappers have been the yard's bread and butter since, but, in the shape of the three-year-old Dazzling Dan, we reckon Sly has her best horse since Speciosa. While it'd be fanciful to expect a return to the top table, we're betting that he can make his mark in some good sprint handicaps in 2019.

Dazzling Dan will start out from a mark of 89, and there's more than one piece of form in the book to suggest that's potentially very lenient. His all-the-way, four-length maiden win at Doncaster on the final day of the turf season impressed both visually and on the clock, while previous seconds to pattern-race performers Watan and Jash (runner-up in the Middle Park) stand up very well, his effort behind the latter at Newmarket coming in one of the hottest novices of the season. Dazzling Dan has raced only at six furlongs so far and, as an enthusiastic, forward-going sort, that's likely to be his trip. He's shown his form on good to firm and good to soft going, but is yet to race on extremes. *Pam Sly*

Conclusion: *Lots of promise in four two-year-old outings and not to be underestimated despite representing a small stable, with an opening mark of 89 looking generous*

Dubai Warrior ★   104p
3 b.c. Dansili – Mahbooba (AUS) (Galileo (Ire))
2018 p8s* Nov 8

The likes of Golden Horn, Kingman and Limato, as well as Calyx and Without Parole last year, have all been flagbearers for the benefits of sectional time analysis, which can be used to identify good or outstanding horses long before they can be recognised as such on form evidence. One of the standout horses on that front amongst the 2018 crop of juveniles was Dubai Warrior, whose debut in a Chelmsford novice event (when sent off a very well-backed 6/5 shot) in November marks him out as potentially high class.

Having been slow to break, he travelled well in mid-field behind the steady early gallop, before making striking headway to lead a furlong out and quickly showing his rivals a clean pair of heels (won by four and a half lengths). The raw timefigure in itself was far from exceptional—though by no means slow—but, when combined with the speed of his closing sectional, it suggests that he's capable of running significantly faster. Indeed, it already puts him close to listed class on that initial performance alone, and he clearly has the potential for plenty of progress as a three-year-old.

His full brother Mootasadir, who only made his debut in April of last year (as a three-year-old), progressed to a Timeform rating of 118 when winning from a BHA mark of 105 on just his seventh start, while his dam was similarly highly rated (116), her wins including the Group 2 Balanchine Stakes at Meydan for Mike de Kock. Mootasadir is currently unbeaten on synthetic surfaces and yet to fully prove his effectiveness on turf, but Mahbooba (their dam), while winning the UAE 1000 Guineas on dirt, is by Galileo and produced her best performances on turf (stayed a mile and a half).

Dubai Warrior is trained by a man with few, if any, peers when it comes to getting a horse to fulfil its potential, and it would come as no surprise were he to join the likes of Enable, Jack Hobbs and Without Parole and become the latest Gosden trainee to make his mark in pattern company having debuted on the all-weather. *John Gosden*

Conclusion: *Made a winning debut in the style of something out of the ordinary and looks sure to progress and win more races; will stay at least 1¼m and makes appeal at 16/1 for the Derby*

Edgewood ·   86p

3 b.c. Garswood – Heskin (Ire) (Acclamation)
2018 7m⁵ 7g² 6d* :: 2019 t6s³ Mar 1

Owner/breeder David Armstrong has long since had a tendency to name his horses after north-west landmarks and/or road names, the villages of Ribchester (in the Ribble Valley), Garswood (near St Helens) and Birchwood (near Warrington) three of the best known, whilst the 2018 Prix de l'Abbaye winner Mabs Cross takes her name from a primary school in Wigan. It's less than five miles driving north west towards the M6 from Mabs Cross to Edgewood and, whilst we're not suggesting that the latter has anything like the potential of Michael Dods' mare, he does strike as another Armstrong home-bred that's more than likely to pay his way in the coming season.

Edgewood improved with each of his three outings in maidens as a two-year-old, dropping down from seven furlongs to six when edging home in a 14-runner event at Doncaster on the final one. Encouragingly, a couple of those behind were successful next-time-out and, even though Edgewood had the benefit of experience over the runner-up that day, he went about things in a likeable fashion, leaving the impression that he's the type to go on again this season. Starting out in handicaps from a BHA mark of 77, he ran creditably when third (beaten just a neck) on his reappearance at Newcastle in March and should prove capable of defying that mark another day, with a return to seven furlongs likely to suit given how strong he was at the finish. *James Bethell*

Conclusion: *Shouldn't have much trouble defying an opening mark which looks on the lenient side before picking up another handicap or two as he progresses with further experience*

Faro Angel (Ire) 93p

3 b.c. Dark Angel (Ire) – Rougette (Red Ransom (USA))
2018 7m⁴ 7m* 8.2d* Oct 16

There was much discussion—and some consternation—within racing circles when it was announced just after winning Newbury's Group 2 Mill Reef Stakes that Kessaar would be retired at the end of his juvenile campaign. It is certainly unusual for two-year-old colts to head straight to stud duties after just one season on the track, though if Kessaar's connections had needed a precedent to justify their actions, then surely Dark Angel—another Mill Reef winner not to race at three and sire of several of this year's *Fifty*, including Faro Angel—would surely be the best example.

Faro Angel didn't see a racecourse until last September but still contributed two of legendary trainer Luca Cumani's six two-year-old wins in his final season with a licence, both coming in 10-runner events at Leicester, the first ultimately achieved only after the stewards correctly decided that Nubough had impeded Faro Angel sufficiently inside the final furlong to affect the result.

A subsequent half-length beating of Laafy also didn't tell the full story of Faro Angel's superiority on the day, his regular jockey Jamie Spencer only doing the minimum that was required to come home in front. Gelded since, and now in the care of an upwardly-mobile trainer, Faro Angel is certainly bred more for speed than stamina, with Dark Angel already responsible for the Group 1-winning sprinters Battaash, Harry Angel, Mecca's Angel and Lethal Force. However, Faro Angel didn't appear to be coming to the end of his tether towards the conclusion of his third start, over an extended mile, and he's certainly one to keep on the right side in handicaps at up to that trip, a physically imposing sort who doesn't appear to have been overburdened with an opening BHA mark of 86. *Charlie Fellowes*

Conclusion: *Won on his last two starts as a two-year-old for Luca Cumani and has the physique to continue his progression into 2019, initially in handicaps*

Feliciana de Vega 100p

3 b.f. Lope de Vega (Ire) – Along Came Casey (Ire) (Oratorio (Ire))
2018 7d* p7.5g* Dec 16

Juana de Guardo, the second wife of Lope de Vega—one of the most famous writers in the history of Spanish literature—died giving birth to her fourth child, Feliciana de Vega. Thankfully for Murry Rose Bloodstock, who own the broodmare Along Came Casey—a dual listed winner up to a mile and a quarter in her racing career with Dermot Weld—the same fate didn't befall the dam of the equine Feliciana de Vega (she has a two-year-old colt by Dark Angel and a yearling foal by Oasis Dream), as her first progeny looks very good indeed.

Strongly backed into odds-on favouritism ahead of her debut at Newmarket in early November, Feliciana de Vega promptly scored by six lengths in a very good time, the inevitable classic quotes swiftly following. It's possible that the filly has since gone a little under the radar, however, with her next run having come on the all-weather track at Deauville in mid-December, when she ran away with the listed Prix des Sablonnets over seven and a half furlongs. Held up towards the rear, she eased closer between horses from halfway before being taken to the outer levelling for home, edging left and still looking a little green but producing a very strong surge to draw clear in the last half-furlong, Christophe Soumillon having given her just one flick of the whip. It might not have been a deep listed race, but it was hard not to be very impressed and everything about her suggests that she's going to be even better as a three-year-old, one who is sure to stay at least a mile. Connections would be well within their rights to think of starting her off in a classic trial and she's very much one to look forward to. **Ralph Beckett**

Conclusion: *Plenty to like about what she did in two juvenile starts and looks an excellent three-year-old prospect, open to significant improvement and sure to win pattern races*

Felix   87p
3 ch.c. Lope de Vega (Ire) – Luminance (Ire) (Danehill Dancer (Ire))
2018 p8g³ 8g* 7.9g² Oct 12

Luca Cumani brought his 43-year training career to an end in December 2018, horses of the quality of Kahyasi, High-Rise, Commanche Run, Barathea and Falbrav having become few and far between in recent times, but the trainer of 45 Group 1 winners will retain more than just a passing interest in horse racing through his ownership of Fittocks Stud, which was purchased in 1984 and has been responsible for numerous good horses over the last three decades. Plenty have been sold, including the likes of the St Leger winner Milan, but plenty have raced successfully in the colours of Fittocks Stud, too, Milan's dam Kithanga winning the Galtres and St Simon Stakes all the way back in 1993.

Felix will be racing in the famous Fittocks Stud silks for Sir Michael Stoute in 2019, having shown considerable promise in three outings for Cumani as a two-year-old, and he appeals as just the sort to develop into a good-quality handicapper (at least) in the forthcoming season. He advanced his form with each start last year, overcoming residual greenness to land a maiden at Yarmouth on his second outing and then progressing again when finding only the similarly promising Sam Cooke (also in the

Fifty) too good under a penalty in a keenly-contested minor event at York in October. An initial BHA mark of 85 is more lenient than might have been anticipated given that Felix seems sure to continue improving for some time yet, his new trainer likely to be at least as adept as the old one in getting the best out of him. Felix, who wears a tongue strap, has raced solely around a mile so far but is bound to be suited by at least another furlong in his second season. **Sir Michael Stoute**

Conclusion: *Just the type of three-year-old that will rise through the handicapping ranks in 2019, likely to be rated a fair bit higher than his current BHA mark of 85 by the season's end*

George of Hearts (Fr)   100

4 gr.g. Kendargent (Fr) – Bugie d'Amore (Rail Link)
2018 p6s* 7f² 8m 8m 6m³ 6g Aug 24

An expensive breeze-up purchase in 2017, George of Hearts still has a fair way to go to repay the €470,000 his owners stumped up for him—his sole win in eight career starts to date came when odds-on for a four-runner Chelmsford maiden on last season's reappearance—but it is what he showed during the remainder of 2018 that warrants his inclusion in our *Fifty*.

George of Hearts took his first step into handicap company at Ascot in May, where he finished a never-nearer half-length second behind the smart Society Power, who coincidentally goes under the name King of Hearts now he's racing in Hong Kong. Society Power—as he was then called—subsequently chased home the future Breeders' Cup Mile-winner Expert Eye in the Jersey Stakes, and, while George of Hearts has come no closer to winning another race since, he begins 2019 with a sense of as yet unfulfilled potential.

George of Hearts again shaped well back at the Berkshire track the following month, this time at the Royal meeting in the Britannia Stakes, where he was dropped out and just too far back to land any meaningful blow, and he probably should have won the Shergar Cup Sprint in August under Swedish jockey Per-Anders Graberg, the effort exerted in rapidly making up plenty of ground from two furlongs out taking its toll late on.

A moderately-run event over Goodwood's straight six-furlong track was never likely to play to George of Hearts's strengths on his final start and, as a still relatively unexposed, smooth-travelling sort who looks fairly versatile regards trip—he's fully effective over a stiff six furlongs and should stay at least a mile—George of Hearts should be able to exploit what remains a fair-looking mark at the start of his 2019 campaign, just the type for something like the Victoria Cup, a race his trainer failed to win as a jockey. **Richard Hughes**

Conclusion: *Yet to add to his Chelmsford maiden success in the early part of 2018, but has shaped well on more than one occasion since and starts this season on a handy mark*

Gravistas   79p

3 b.c. Dansili – Gaze (Galileo (Ire))
2018 p8d⁶ t8.6g² 10s² Oct 8

It would be remiss to compile a *Fifty* such as this without including at least one Mark Johnston-trained three-year-old handicapper, and Gravistas looks a prime candidate to improve plenty this year.

His pedigree automatically piques interest. His dam, though no great shakes on the racecourse, is closely related to the top-class Fame And Glory, and she has already produced a smart horse in the form of the Luca Cumani-trained Greatwood, as well as several other fairly useful sorts, most of them excelling over a mile and a half-plus (the only one who didn't subsequently winning over hurdles). On top of that, Dansili, though versatile, has sired his very best performers over middle-distances, so the pedigree is clearly there for Gravistas to progress as his stamina is drawn out.

Three quickfire runs towards the back end of his two-year-old season (improved a little with each of them) saw Gravistas acquire experience, and the way he shaped on his final start in a minor event at Pontefract cemented the impression that he will have more to offer when going up in trip; in a well-run race, he was in the heat of battle much sooner than the winner and kept on well with that in mind to be beaten only a length and three quarters, with another 11 lengths back to the third.

The China Horse Club has quickly made a big impact on the international thoroughbred scene through the likes of the 2018 American Triple Crown winner Justify, and, while we're not suggesting Gravistas is going to be one of their stars, he's certainly a horse who could represent them at the big festivals, with the likes of the King George V Handicap at Royal Ascot and the Melrose at York appealing as potential targets, with the scope from his current mark to win a couple of northern handicaps early in the season en route. ***Mark Johnston***

Conclusion: *Improved with racing as a two-year-old and appeals as the type to continue in a similar vein in 2019, especially when going up in trip (likely to stay at least 1½m)*

 facebook.com/timeform1948

Happy Power (Ire) 99p

3 gr.c. Dark Angel (Ire) – Tamarisk (Ger) (Selkirk (USA))
2018 6m⁴ 6d* 6s³ 7g* Oct 27

2018 was the year when horses carrying the predominantly-blue silks of King Power Racing became an increasing presence on racecourses, both in Britain and abroad. The standard-bearer was the dual Group 2-winning miler Beat The Bank, though it would be no surprise if he was surpassed in 2019 by one of their many promising two-year-olds from last season, including his stablemate Happy Power, for whom it was very much a campaign of progression.

Having shaped encouragingly when fourth on his debut at Newbury in May, Happy Power showed improved form to justify favouritism at Hamilton three months later, readily drawing clear from two furlongs out to win by two and three quarter lengths. A return visit to the Scottish venue in September failed to yield a second success, though Happy Power didn't get the rub of the green on the day (endured a troubled passage) and ultimately did well under the circumstances to get within a length and a half of the subsequent Group 3 winner (and Breeders' Cup Juvenile Fillies Turf runner-up)

Andrew Balding has enjoyed plenty of success with horses carrying the King Power silks

East. There were no such traffic problems on Happy Power's final outing of the season, when he took advantage of a lenient opening mark to run away with a six-runner nursery at Doncaster.

Happy Power is speedily bred but seemed to relish the step up to seven furlongs on Town Moor, which will provide connections with more options distance-wise for the upcoming campaign, and while there are certainly more handicaps to be won in 2019, it may be that Happy Power is on a path heading towards group races before the year is out. *Andrew Balding*

Conclusion: *Speedily-bred sort who showed progressive form as a juvenile and seems sure to improve further as a three-year-old, initially in handicaps, though it'll be no surprise if he's competing in pattern races before the end of the campaign*

Hero Hero (Ire) 89p

3 b.c. No Nay Never (USA) – Fancy (Ire) (Galileo (Ire))
2018 6d² Nov 10

It must have been a blow to her connections that Fancy never made it to the track given how well-related she is, by Galileo and out of the Group 3 winner Danehill Music, making her a full sister to the year-younger Seussical, who only raced seven times but was well on his way to becoming a very smart middle-distance performer before his career ended prematurely. Nevertheless, there is at least time for Fancy to show her worth in the paddocks, and the early signs are very encouraging, with her first foal Hero Hero having made a debut full of promise at Doncaster last November.

Sent off the 7/2 favourite in a 14-runner maiden over six furlongs, Hero Hero may have failed to meet market expectations when chasing home fellow *Fifty* member Edgewood, but he went like the best horse at the weights on the day, the only one to make the frame without prior experience and coming from further back than ideal, a view supported by time analysis. His sectional upgrade of 14 lb was at least 5 lb superior to anything else in the line-up and, when coupled with the fair timefigure, gives real substance to the performance, with further lustre added by the fifth and seventh that day both improving appreciably to score next-time-out.

Hero Hero is by speed influence No Nay Never, but he should stay at least seven furlongs on the balance of his pedigree, and looks a banker to open his account sooner rather than later, a useful prospect at the very least for 2019. *Andrew Balding*

Conclusion: *Showed plenty when filling the runner-up spot on his debut and should find a similar event well within his range before graduating to handicaps for his excellent yard*

Hummdinger (Fr)

61p

3 ch.g. Planteur (Ire) – Interior (USA) (Fusaichi Pegasus (USA))
2018 7m 7m⁶ p8g⁴ Sep 25

The origins of the quote 'nothing is certain except death and taxes' has historically been open to question, perhaps most commonly attributed to Benjamin Franklin—one of the founding fathers of the United States—in a 1789 letter to French scientist Jean-Baptiste Leroy after the signing of the emerging nation's first Constitution. There have been many variations on that theme over the years and recent subscribers to this publication might be tempted to tag on 'and an unexposed, Alan King-trained three-year-old featuring in the Flat *Fifty*', given that such a horse is included in these pages for the third year in succession.

Just In Time has scaled the heights since appearing in the 2017 edition, winning three times in each of the last two seasons, and while it would be somewhat tempting on our part to draw a veil over the fact that Nebuchadnezzar remains a maiden after an abbreviated 2018 campaign, that doesn't diminish our hopes for Hummdinger, whose profile setting out on his second season of racing bears a striking resemblance to those of the aforementioned duo.

It's pretty obvious that the surface has barely been scratched so far as Hummdinger is concerned, with races over seven furlongs on good to firm going (at Sandown and Leicester), and then over a mile on Lingfield's all-weather track, merely steps on a path that seems likely to feature handicaps over longer trips before too long. His pedigree certainly suggests as much—he is by Planteur, a very smart middle-distance performer in his day, and out of the unraced mare Interior, who is herself a half-sister to the prolific Be Perfect, a winner over as far as two and a quarter miles.

There is clearly an element of guesswork as to what level Hummdinger will eventually ascend to, but the early groundwork has been done and—as Franklin might have written—he seems certain to show much more with time and distance in 2019. **Alan King**

Conclusion: *Made little impact in a brief two-year-old campaign, but has scope for appreciable second-season improvement, starting out in low-grade handicaps from a BHA mark of 62*

Ibraz

103+

4 b.c. Farhh – Wadaa (USA) (Dynaformer (USA))
2018 7d³ 8.3m* 9g* 8g Jul 14

Handicappers who start their four-year-old campaign with little racing behind them and the potential to do better still are often worth following, especially ones who are likely to be contesting higher-end events where the weight-for-age allowance means that three-year-olds struggle to get a run, and Ibraz looks to fit that bill.

After just one start as a juvenile, Ibraz made a promising reappearance when third in a Newmarket maiden in April and duly progressed again to break his duck in a minor event at Nottingham the following month, readily seeing off a trio of rivals who developed into useful types later that season, including fellow member of the *Fifty* Infrastructure.

Strong in the market for his handicap bow at Sandown in June, he justified that confidence to follow up and, though only workmanlike on the day (won by a neck), it proved to be a strong piece of form; the runner-up Gossip Column and third Kassar both won next-time-out, while the fourth-placed Hasanoanda added two more wins to his tally before the end of 2018, improving by the thick end of a stone in the process.

Ibraz proved a disappointment on his final start at Newmarket, when managing only seventh, but his subsequent absence suggests all may not have been well that day, and whilst that would ordinarily be a slight concern heading into his four-year-old campaign, an entry in the Lincoln suggests that he's over whatever ailed him that day and is ready to roll for 2019. He's unlikely to get into that race off a BHA mark of 93, but the consolation Spring Mile looks an ideal starting point for what could be a coming-of-age season. **Roger Varian**

Conclusion: *Clearly not himself in last season's hat-trick bid and expected to get back on the up this time round, with big handicaps at around 1m likely to feature highly on his agenda*

Imperial Court (Ire)   83p
4 b.g. Zoffany (Ire) – La Vita Bella (Mtoto)
2018 8.2g⁶ p13.3g⁴ 11.8m⁴ p12s² p12d² Nov 23

Zoffany's career on the track was a case of 'close but not quite'—a successful juvenile, winning five of his seven starts, he failed to really build on that promise at three, with his most renowned moment coming when pushing Frankel closer than any other horse managed in 2011 in the St James's Palace Stakes, albeit grossly flattered in the process. His performance at stud has followed a similar path, with the early promise shown by the likes of Foundation and Architecture having quickly fizzled out, but we expect the career of another of his progeny, Imperial Court, to burn brightly in 2019.

Admittedly, Imperial Court is starting out from a much lower base than those previously mentioned, but his performances on the track to date have been filled with promise, brought along gradually in novice company before stepping up on his two handicap starts, twice finishing second at Kempton. On the first occasion, Imperial Court shaped well behind a progressive rival, and he went like the best horse at the weights on his latest outing, finding himself poorly placed and forced to concede first run to the winner who benefited from an excellent Adam Kirby ride. A handicap mark of 68 is modest in comparison with most in this publication, but that is what makes Imperial Court an ideal horse to follow, likely to fly under the radar of many, and we fully expect him to make a sizeable leap up the handicap ranks this term. **David Simcock**

Conclusion: *Remains a maiden after five starts, but took his form to a new level in two starts in handicaps; one to note with further improvement on the cards (will stay beyond 1½m)*

Infrastructure   100p

4 ch.g. Raven's Pass (USA) – Foundation Filly (Lando (Ger))
2018 8d⁶ 10.3g² 8.3m³ 9.9g² 12m* 12g⁶ 12d⁶ Sep 21

Martyn Meade first started training racehorses in the 1970s, but it is only in the last five seasons that he has taken his success to the next level, coinciding with the move to Sefton Lodge in Newmarket in 2014. During his time at Flat racing's headquarters, he sent out 66 winners from only 429 runners (strike-rate of over 15%) and enjoyed his first Group 1 success courtesy of Aclaim in the 2017 Prix de la Foret at Chantilly. Shortly after this success, Meade expanded his operation significantly with the purchase of the main part of Manton Stables in Wiltshire, and his intentions were rewarded during his first season at his new base, with Advertise—owned by the big-spending Phoenix Thoroughbreds—giving the yard a second Group 1 when winning the Phoenix Stakes at the Curragh.

2019 looks set to be another bright year for the Meade stable, and it'd be a surprise if Infrastructure didn't pick up at least a couple of handicaps for the cause as a four-year-old. Infrastructure won only one of his seven starts in 2018, but he emerged with some really strong form to his name, notably when splitting Chief Ironside and Argentello (now Timeform-rated 111 and 112, respectively) in a maiden at Chester in May, and when beating a host of improvers in a warm three-year-old handicap at Salisbury in June. Infrastructure's form tailed off a bit after that success, but that's no negative overall, given that he was coming to the end of just his first spell of racing (didn't race as a two-year-old), and he has the physique (strong gelding) to expect even more from him as a four-year-old, a middle-distance handicap likely to be his for the taking from his current BHA mark of 90. **Martyn Meade**

Conclusion: *Has some strong three-year-old form to his name and looks the type to progress further as a four-year-old*

 Follow us on Twitter @Timeform

Khaadem looks a sprinter to follow this season

Khaadem (Ire)   110p

3 br.c. Dark Angel (Ire) – White Daffodil (Ire) (Footstepsinthesand)
2018 6g³ 6g* 6g* Sep 12

When Battaash ran away with the King George Stakes at last season's Qatar Goodwood Festival ('Glorious' Goodwood as was), it was rated by Timeform as the best performance seen at any distance in Britain in 2018, only subsequently surpassed by Cracksman's demolition job in the Champion Stakes.

Khaadem—like Battaash a Hamdan Al Maktoum-owned, Charles Hills-trained son of Dark Angel—raced too freely when finishing third in a Newmarket maiden on his debut in June, that race won by fellow newcomer Calyx, who just ten days later followed-up in the Coventry Stakes at Royal Ascot. Reportedly struck into that day, it was another 10 weeks before Khaadem made his second start, again on the July Course, where he more than confirmed that debut promise, impressively quickening clear from seven rivals. He then carried his progression through to his final start at Doncaster, where he produced a useful effort to follow up, despite again doing a fair bit wrong, keen to get on with things in the early stages but keeping on well to beat another previous winner, Swissterious, by a length and a quarter.

Khaadem looks all about speed, no surprise in that given his pedigree, a full brother to Log Out Island, who won Redcar's Two-Year-Old Trophy in his juvenile campaign and finished first past the post in the listed Carnarvon Stakes at Newbury the following May, only to be later disqualified after testing positive for a banned substance. That particular race seems likely to be on the radar of Khaadem's connections if, as anticipated, he bypasses the early season Guineas trials, and it's not difficult to visualize him developing into a pattern-race performer before too long, perhaps even a contender for the fifth running of the Commonwealth Cup, a race that provided the first of four straight Group 1 victories for the same connections' top-class sprinter Muhaarar in 2015. **Charles Hills**

Conclusion: *Speedy sort who improved with each run in a three-race juvenile campaign, winning on his last two starts; looks the sort to develop into a Group-race performer at sprint distances in 2019*

Lah Ti Dar ★   122

4 b.f. Dubawi (Ire) – Dar Re Mi (Singspiel (Ire))
2018 10d* 10m* 11.9m* 14.5g^2 12d^3 Oct 20

The Super Bowl is the annual championship game of the NFL and the Holy Grail of American sports, surpassing ice hockey's Stanley Cup or baseball's World Series. It's estimated that more than 9,000 college students take to the field in the US every year to start their path towards a potential career in the pros, though only a fraction succeed—the latest NFL Draft saw only 256 players taken through its seven-round

Lah Ti Dar annihalates her rivals in a listed race at York's Ebor Festival

process. This rarefied sporting air makes the odds of a fledgling player reaching the Super Bowl astronomical, so for two from the same family—twin brothers Devin and Jason McCoutry—to achieve the feat, and indeed win the coveted prize with the New England Patriots, during the latest season, was something that probably won't ever be repeated.

In the interests of modesty (and realism!), Timeform isn't the NFL, and *Horses To Follow* isn't the Super Bowl, but, much like the McCourtys, a pair of siblings are set to feature heavily in the long-running publication's success. Fellow *Fifty* member Too Darn Hot is the 'talking horse' of the pair in question, courtesy of a blistering juvenile campaign, but look to year-older sister Lah Ti Dar to take the middle-distance scene by storm in 2019. Granted, Lah Ti Dar failed to hit the expected heights when sent off the evens favourite on Champions Day for her final appearance of last year, but she'd done so much good work prior to that display—notably a ten-length rout of a listed field at York in August that will live long in the memory for its visual impression—that it doesn't take great powers of forgiveness to give her a pass for Ascot, which, after all, had come only five weeks after a massive effort in the St Leger (clear second to Kew Gardens).

Lah Ti Dar was robbed of her first shot at classic success—her St Leger defeat came after an unsatisfactory blood picture had forced her to miss the Oaks—but she can make amends in some of the major all-aged prizes this time around. *John Gosden*

Conclusion: *Did her bit for one of the best racing bloodlines in the book in her first season and can take her form up another notch with another year on her back*

 # Ledham (Ire) 99p
4 b.c. Shamardal (USA) – Pioneer Bride (USA) (Gone West (USA))
2018 7m² t7.2s* 8g² p8s* p8d³ Oct 16

There's no better trainer around at executing a 'softly, softly' approach than Sir Michael Stoute, and when the master of Freemason Lodge keeps an expensive, big, rangy individual in training for a third season, it's time to sit up and take notice.

Ledham made it to the course only once as a two-year-old and was easy to back before running green in a seven-furlong maiden at Sandown, nonetheless showing no small amount of promise and earning himself a Timeform large 'P'. There was still lingering greenness when he reappeared with a second-placed finish at Lingfield last May, but he remained in plenty of punters' notebooks and was backed off the boards at Wolverhampton less than three weeks later, when ultimately winning with authority from the front. Three more second-season outings in handicaps yielded only a single further success for Ledham, in a mile handicap, also on the all-weather at Kempton, but, perhaps more significantly, the pattern of gradual improvement continued.

Ledham has been entered in the Lincoln Handicap at Doncaster, but looks unlikely to get a run as things stand—it took a BHA mark of 97 to guarantee a place in last year's line-up, and he is currently down on 89. There is always the Spring Mile on the same card, though, a race which the Sir Michael Stoute-trained Ballet Concerto, who also sported the blue and yellow colours of Mr Saeed Suhail, won in 2017. He went on to improve the best part of a stone in the second half of that season, claiming further success in the John Smith's Cup at York, the Group 3 Sovereign Stakes at Salisbury and the Superior Mile, another Group 3, at Haydock—we'll be keeping our fingers firmly crossed that Ledham can scale similar heights in 2019. **Sir Michael Stoute**

Conclusion: *Big, rangy sort who improved with racing last season and looks sure to do better again this time round with another winter under his belt*

Lord Oberon ★ 109p

4 b.g. Mayson – Fairy Shoes (Kyllachy)
2018 f7.1g* p7d^4 f6.1m* 7d^2 6m^2 6s^2 7d* Nov 10

2019 will mark the tenth anniversary of Lord Shanakill's win in the Prix Jean Prat at Chantilly, which provided trainer Karl Burke with his first Group 1 success. It would be another six years before Burke achieved further success at the top level thanks to Odeliz, the intervening period somewhat chequered for the master of Spigot Lodge, but since then the achievements of Quiet Reflection, Unfortunately and most notably Laurens, who amongst her glittering three-year-old campaign provided Burke with a first classic win (Prix de Diane), have further raised the profile of his Middleham yard.

Lord Oberon still has a fair way to go to be mentioned in the same breath as the above-mentioned horses, but he maintained a largely upward trajectory throughout his first season of racing. Having failed to make the track as a two-year-old, we didn't have long to wait to see him in 2018, belying his inexperience as the only unraced runner in the field to edge out main market rival Kripke in a novice event at Southwell in the first half of January. A second visit to the Nottinghamshire venue less than three months later reaped further reward and, by the time that Lord Oberon had made it three wins for the year at Doncaster on the final day of turf racing in Britain in November (overcoming some trouble in-running and finding plenty to eventually reel in Cold Stare entering the final hundred yards), he had already developed into a useful performer at both six and seven furlongs.

Lord Oberon looks just the type to progress further as a four-year-old, his immediate future surely in top-end handicaps, where he should certainly make his presence felt, still unexposed and seemingly versatile regards both ground and racing surface.
Karl Burke

Conclusion: *Lightly-raced performer who ended his three-year-old campaign with a career-best success at Doncaster, having gone close on all three previous starts in handicaps; looks the type to progress further in 2019*

Simon Baker, Senior Horse Racing Analyst (Lord Oberon): *"Lord Oberon was versatile, straightforward, consistent and progressive in 2018 and there's surely lots more to come after just seven lifetime starts. Expect those qualities to serve him well again this season, when he'll hopefully be a fixture in all the top handicaps between six furlongs and a mile."*

Magical Spirit (Ire)   79p

3 ch.g. Zebedee – La Dame de Fer (Ire) (Mr Greeley (USA))
2018 5d 5m³ 5d* Sep 25

The case for Magical Spirit is a straightforward one. He showed progressive form in three minor events at Beverley, all over the minimum trip, as a two-year-old and, not only will he start life in handicaps from a potentially favourable BHA mark of 71, but he gives the strong impression he'll continue improving in his second season.

Magical Spirit still wasn't the finished article by any means when winning the last of those three starts (hung left when hitting the front), but he did knuckle down well for pressure and the form of the race worked out rather better than might have been expected, albeit at an ordinary level. Gelded over the winter, the simple fact he was kept away from artificial surfaces suggests connections harbour greater aspirations for him than just picking up the odd everyday handicap on the all-weather. Magical Spirit has raced solely over five furlongs to date and the likelihood is that he'll be nothing other than a sprinter, at least for the foreseeable future, just the sort his stable will continue to improve for a while yet. *Kevin Ryan*

Conclusion: *Starts life in handicaps from a potentially lenient mark and looks sure to win more races if his trainer's record with similar types is anything to go by*

Marronnier (Ire)   86p

3 ch.g. Lope de Vega (Ire) – Beach Bunny (Ire) (High Chaparral (Ire))
2018 7d³ 7.4g⁴ 7d* Oct 9

A rare public appearance by the legendary gambler Patrick Veitch on a February 2019 edition of the popular Racing TV vehicle 'Luck On Sunday' probably had most dyed-in-the-wool harking back to a Nottingham maiden in October 2004. The race was run under the name "Wright Brothers Maiden Stakes", and there was plenty of invention involved in the perfectly-executed gamble on the Veitch-owned Exponential, whose opening price of 100/1 had tumbled to 8/1 by the time the stalls opened. There was barely any doubt about the outcome in the race, netting Veitch a healthy share of the reported £500,000 winnings.

That famous gamble played a part in forging Stuart Williams' reputation as one of the shrewder operators on the Flat scene, though the stable's recent totals point to a yard that's an entirely different proposition nowadays—one less about the talk of gambles and plots and more about the accumulation of winners. Exponential was one of Williams' then joint-best seasonal haul of 32 back in 2004, a total he's equalled or surpassed for the last six years, culminating in the leap to 58 during the latest campaign.

Williams' improvement has brought with it the 'honour' of a representative in this year's *Fifty* in the shape of Marronnier, a clear-cut winner of a Brighton maiden on the last of his three starts as a two-year-old. The first two were marked by Marronnier's inexperience, as slow starts left him on the back foot, but he'd flashed home at Beverley on the second of them and duly built on that promise as he put it all together on his 2018 swansong, a performance most notable for his strength up the closing hill.

Marronnier has raced only around seven furlongs, but the way he's shaped—and indeed is bred, by stamina-influence Lope de Vega and out of a winner over a mile and a quarter—firmly suggests that he'll flourish over longer distances in handicaps in 2019. **Stuart Williams**

Conclusion: *Represents a yard on the rise and signed off as a juvenile with a maiden success that hinted strongly towards further improvement in handicaps at 1m and beyond*

Mulan (Ire)   75p

3 b.f. Kingman – Platonic (Zafonic (USA))
2018 6g 6g⁶ p6d⁶ Oct 16

In many ways, Mulan is the archetypal *Horses To Follow* candidate. Expensive purchase with a pedigree to match? Check. With a top yard? Check. Goes into a three-year-old campaign after three quickfire qualifying runs over an inadequate trip? Check.

Joining these dots in more detail gives even more cause for encouragement, though. A €300,000 purchase by crack miler Kingman but with a stamina-laden distaff side (half-sister to several winners, including a Group 3-winning stayer and a couple of other useful middle-distance winners), Mulan's juvenile form was more than just a grounding for her three-year-old campaign, with the form of her third outing having plenty of substance to it, too.

After a couple of runs at Yarmouth where her inexperience was apparent, Mulan was kept to six furlongs at Kempton and offered plenty to work on in finishing six lengths behind Red Impression, with her rider never getting that animated after she had met some trouble at a critical stage (just as she was gathering momentum). The winner that day followed up impressively at Lingfield and has also made the *Fifty*, whilst the second and fourth home also improved when scoring next-time-out.

With a mile sure to suit, Mulan looks banker material from an opening BHA mark of 72 and could easily be the type to rack up a few wins as she climbs the handicap ranks, either in fillies' contests or when mixing it with the boys, and, all in all, it looks as if the Stoute team have got one to go to war with in 2019. *Sir Michael Stoute*

Conclusion: *Went through the motions in three two-year-old starts, but the foundations are there for one who should prove a different proposition when going up in trip in handicaps*

Nearooz   88p
3 b.f. New Approach (Ire) – Modeyra (Shamardal (USA))
2018 7m* Oct 12

Trying to find a genuine Oaks candidate at this time of year is a risky business, as current odds of 16/1 bar suggest, with any number of unexposed, well-bred sorts in the entries. However, we're happy to suggest Nearooz as one with the potential to scale those heights, and, if she doesn't quite measure up to that exalted level, we still expect her to develop into a genuine pattern-class horse over middle-distances this season.

Nearooz made it to the track just once as a juvenile, but it was a winning start, showing a good attitude to take a seven-furlong Newmarket maiden in October, edging out next-time-out winner Watheerah by a short head and catching the eye of our sectional timings team in the process (her upgrade coupled with the overall timefigure is indicative of one already capable of decidedly useful form). Sent off at 20/1, that debut performance seemingly came as a surprise to her connections, but they can be forgiven if they have much bigger aspirations for her in 2019.

By New Approach and out of a listed winner over a mile and a quarter (herself out of a Nassau Stakes winner), Nearooz is bred in the purple and, as a rather unfurnished type as a juvenile, she appeals as the type to have done well over the winter, too. She'll deserve to be high on the shortlist if turning up in an Oaks trial for her reappearance, and though her future path rather depends on how that initial step up goes, she's clearly very much one to look forward to. *Roger Varian*

Conclusion: *Displayed a willing attitude to spring a surprise in a back-end Newmarket maiden and could well make up into an Oaks contender, current odds of 33/1 looking attractive*

Outbox   110p

4 b.g. Frankel – Emirates Queen (Street Cry (Ire))
2018 12m* 11.8m* 13.3d* Oct 26

Being by Frankel and out of Emirates Queen—the Lancashire Oaks winner who is a half-sister to Dubawi—Outbox has claims of being one of the best-bred horses in training, certainly a potentially hugely valuable commodity as a stallion, so the fact that he made his debut in the September of his three-year-old season having already been gelded suggests that he must not have been the most straightforward as a young horse. However, while understandably a little green on his debut, there was nothing in his three runs—all wins—last year to suggest that he is anything other than a really likeable performer, and he rates an exciting prospect for pattern races in 2019.

After staying on strongly to beat Spirit Ridge (who went on to see off a good field of three-year-old handicappers on his next start) over a mile and a half on his debut at Ffos Las, Outbox was able to control matters in a similar event at Leicester next time, only having to be pushed out to see off a lightly-raced Godolphin filly, the pair of them coming well clear of the rest. It was his final run, though, in a valuable three-year-old conditions race over a mile and five furlongs at Newbury in October, that really marks him down as one to follow.

Sent off favourite to beat a couple with smart form already in the book, a steady gallop threatened to catch him out up against more experienced rivals, his greenness apparent when the tempo started to lift half a mile out, but his talent shone through, fighting his way to the front inside the final furlong and ultimately winning a shade more comfortably than the official winning margin would suggest. A powerful galloper, the style of that success suggests that he'll be even better when going up in trip, and with both his sire and dam proving better at four, he's very much the type to come into his own this year, the potential there for him to develop into a 'Cup' horse. *Simon Crisford*

Conclusion: *Lightly-raced sort who gained plenty of admirers when maintaining his unbeaten record at Newbury in the autumn; looks sure to be plying his trade in pattern events in 2019, with the best undoubtedly yet to come (will stay beyond 1¾m)*

Private Secretary   89p

3 b.c. Kingman – Intrigued (Darshaan)
2018 7d² 8.3s² Nov 7

It's not hard to come up with reasons as to why Private Secretary will develop into an above-average three-year-old. Well backed ahead of his debut (usually a telling sign for newcomers from the Gosden yard), Private Secretary produced a fairly useful effort to fill the runner-up spot in a novice event at Yarmouth, one that contained several well-bred individuals from big yards and has worked out well, with the third and the seventh both taking big steps forward to win next-time-out.

For his part, Private Secretary could only take a sideways step when also finishing second on his next start at Nottingham, but there was plenty to like about the way he went through the contest, pulling clear of the rest and still looking one who can win races. Indeed, the future is likely to show that there was no disgrace in finishing two and a quarter lengths behind the very promising Space Blues, another member of this year's *Fifty* and one who has the potential to go to the very top.

By Kingman and out of the useful mare Intrigued, the majority of Private Secretary's siblings have stayed a mile and a half, notably the smart performer Michelangelo (who stayed a mile and three quarters) and Chester Cup winner No Heretic, and it's over middle-distances that Private Secretary should flourish for his top stable as a three-year-old. *John Gosden*

Conclusion: *Well-bred colt who showed plenty in both juvenile starts and seems sure to improve for the step up to middle-distances*

Red Impression   110p

3 gr.f. Dark Angel (Ire) – Purissima (USA) (Fusaichi Pegasus (USA))
2018 p6d* p6g* Nov 24

Roger Charlton had to wait until the second half of September for a winning two-year-old debutant in 2018, but three others quickly followed, all of them well touted in the market and looking exciting prospects, none more so than Red Impression. The bare time of her win at Kempton in October was just modest, but her closing sectional was anything but, and it could easily have been even quicker. Indeed, it was noticeable that jockey Kieran Shoemark was happy to bide his time when a gap first emerged between the leaders just under two furlongs out, clearly aware of what his filly was capable of, and the manner in which she quickened clear meant that the rest of us soon were, too. At Lingfield five weeks later, Red Impression had the platform on which to express herself all the more thanks to the free-going Journey of Life, who soon had the field well strung out, and that's exactly what she did, lowering the two-year-old course record without coming in for anything like a hard ride, once again clocking a notably quick closing sectional.

Several winners have emerged from both her races, underpinning the deeply impressive things that she had been doing on the clock, and it's hard to know what her limit might be. Clearly, she has to prove herself on turf, but there's nothing in her pedigree to suggest that she won't act on it, and while the temptation is always there to step up in trip early in a promising juvenile's three-year-old season, it would be no surprise if connections opted to stick at six furlongs in the immediate future, such is the speed she possesses. *Roger Charlton*

Conclusion: *Exciting prospect who didn't need to show all that she is capable of in winning both her starts at two and appeals as a bona fide contender for top-level sprint honours this season*

Rocket Action   96p

3 b.c. Toronado (Ire) – Winning Express (Ire) (Camacho)
2018 5.1d³ t5s* Nov 22

No matter which operation they come from, juveniles very often leave their debut form behind second-time-out, and Robert Cowell's two-year-olds are no different, with the median improvement that they showed between their first and second runs in 2018 standing at 6 lb on Timeform ratings. The median is a good way to gauge sample data containing outliers, and Rocket Action is a perfect example of a Cowell-trained horse who bucked the trend in this instance—indeed, his performance rating on his second start came in at a whopping 36 lb higher than on his debut.

It was hard to rate Rocket Action's first start at Windsor particularly highly, given that the race was won by Aegean Mist, who'd been beaten off BHA marks in the low-60s in nurseries, but Rocket Action did show definite ability amidst greenness as he kept on for third having been outpaced a couple of furlongs out. He looked a much more professional model on his second start, which came on the tapeta at Newcastle, travelling well just off the pace before quickening to lead inside the final two furlongs and putting good distance between himself and the rest late on. The form of that race is nothing special (though the second did win a nursery in December), but the time was solid enough and there's a good chance that Rocket Action is flying into his second season slightly under the radar. **Robert Cowell**

Conclusion: *Showed huge improvement from his first run to his second and looks a speedy three-year-old in the making*

Sam Cooke (Ire)   86p

3 b.g. Pour Moi (Ire) – Saturday Girl (Peintre Celebre (USA))
2018 p8d² p8g² 7.9g* Oct 12

Anyone who suffered from boredom—and there were surely many—during British racing's equine flu-enforced shutdown could have done worse than spin through the many variations of ownership group names under the Chelsea Thoroughbred banner, before attempting to guess the horse based on the chosen moniker. The prominent racing club opted for 'Chelsea Thoroughbreds—The Sweeney' for their recent recruit Jack Regan, named after John Thaw's character in the hit police drama, while acting legends Tony Curtis and Humphrey Bogart—whose equine namesakes both reached a smart level for the syndicate—were covered by the clever addition of 'Saint Tropez'.

Choosing the supplementary line for Sam Cooke, Chelsea Syndicate's representative in the latest of edition of this publication, might well have provided the biggest headache of them all, however, given the vast discography attached to the singer in whose honour the horse was named.

Ultimately, 'Wonderful World' might prove a smart choice should Sam Cooke make the impact that's expected of him in three-year-old handicaps this year.

Sam Cooke got off the mark at the third attempt with some comfort when taking care of 15 rivals in a minor event at York in October, relishing the switch to turf following a pair of seconds at Kempton and Lingfield the previous month. His win, like his first two outings, came over a mile, but he's very much bred for middle-distances and, what's more, he boasts more than enough physical scope to think he'll train on well. *Ralph Beckett*

Conclusion: *Made a solid start to his career in a light autumn campaign, but promises to really excel once upped in trip in handicaps in 2019*

San Donato (Ire) ★ 115p

3 b.c. Lope de Vega (Ire) – Boston Rocker (Ire) (Acclamation)
2018 6m² 7m 6g* p6g* 6g* Oct 27

Roger Varian isn't afraid to take the patient approach with his horses and it has rarely paid off more than in the second half of 2018, when a pair of last year's *Fifty* belatedly lived up to the high hopes that had been held for them—the four-year-old Sharja Bridge won the extremely valuable Balmoral Handicap on only his ninth career start, while his year-older stablemate Zabeel Prince was even less experienced when narrowly losing out in the Joel Stakes at Newmarket earlier in the autumn, producing a career best on just his eighth racecourse appearance.

With that in mind, there was something quite unusual about the way that San Donato—like Sharja Bridge and Zabeel Prince owned by Sheikh Mohammed Obaid Al Maktoum—was campaigned during the early part of his juvenile season in 2018; he was pitched into the Chesham Stakes at Royal Ascot, just 31 days after his debut second (when showing plenty of greenness) at Yarmouth. The Chesham ultimately came too early for San Donato—he was green and noisy in the preliminaries and still in need of the experience during the race—but, after a mid-season break, he showed why the normally-patient Varian had upped him in grade so quickly after his debut, progressing rapidly as he went unbeaten in three autumn starts.

San Donato began by winning a deep-looking novice at Haydock, beating a whole host of improvers, including the subsequent Group 2 winner Hello Youmzain, and he then made light work of defying a penalty at Kempton three weeks later, looking a much more professional model by that stage. San Donato then won the listed Doncaster Stakes on his final start of the campaign, improving another chunk in the process.

San Donato (spots on cap) completes the hat-trick in comfortable fashion on Town Moor

Connections will surely have a Commonwealth Cup trial in mind for him to begin his three-year-old campaign, and we are likely to see a much different San Donato at Royal Ascot this time around, with current odds of around 20/1 for that race making some appeal at this stage. **Roger Varian**

Conclusion: *Improved in leaps and bounds towards the end of his juvenile campaign, displaying an impressive turn of foot, and could make up into Commonwealth Cup contender*

Sh Boom   83p
3 b.f. War Command (USA) – Nouvelle Lune (Fantastic Light (USA))
2018 7m⁵ 8d* Sep 22

No Nay Never was the undoubted star amongst last year's crop of first-season sires, leading the way in Britain and Ireland in terms of both individual winners (22) and total prize money won (£836,960). However, another Coolmore sire, War Command, quietly went about compiling a very solid record of his own, with 16 winners from only 39 runners (41% strike-rate), and there is seemingly plenty to look forward to with his progeny in 2019, not least with Sh Boom, who looks sure to have more to offer as she sets out on her three-year-old campaign.

A half-sister to the useful pair Maverick (winner up to a mile and a quarter) and Pleasure Dome (stays a mile and three quarters), Sh Boom very much caught the eye when fifth on her debut in a seven-furlong minor event at Goodwood in September, forced to come from further back than ideal in a slowly-run race and doing well under the circumstances to finish as close as she did, beaten a little over five lengths but likely to have given the first two a race on a level playing field. Three of the four who beat her that day went on to contest the Oh So Sharp Stakes at Newmarket in October, and they all finished in the first quartet once again—albeit in a different order—with Mot Juste (fourth at Goodwood) taking a significant step forward to get the verdict.

Sh Boom had already done her own bit to advertise the form by that stage, having confirmed her debut promise to win a minor event at Newmarket 18 days later. Upped in trip by a furlong, she was always travelling strongly in the leaders' slipstream and found plenty when asked for her effort over a furlong out, edging to the front close home (won by a short head).

Both her pedigree and the way that she has shaped in her two starts to date suggest that Sh Boom will be suited by middle-distances in 2019. She still needs one more run to qualify for a handicap mark, but it would be no surprise if she proved a bit better than that, in truth, and connections will likely have designs on getting some black type with her. Either way, she looks well up to winning more races in the months ahead. *Peter Chapple-Hyam*

Conclusion: *Built on considerable debut promise when winning at Newmarket and should progress further when tackling middle-distances as a three-year-old*

Sir Ron Priestley   87p

3 ch.c. Australia – Reckoning (Ire) (Danehill Dancer (Ire))
2018 7.4m^2 8m^4 Sep 4

Mark Johnston became the most successful trainer in the history of British racing during the 2018 season, and it was rather fitting that it was a horse of Poet's Society's profile who broke the record for him—remarkably, the four-year-old was making his 26th start of the season when producing a career best to win at York's Ebor Festival, with that victory coming only six days after a one-paced fifth on the all-weather at Chelmsford. The yard's aggressive style of campaigning their runners is clearly one that works for them, but it is also one that makes including Johnston-trained horses in the *Fifty* a risky proposition. And, whilst it's not recommended to back our *Fifty* blind whatever the circumstances, we are keeping our fingers firmly crossed that Sir Ron Priestley does not emulate King of Macedon's 2014 season, in which he went winless in 15 starts and ended up with a Timeform squiggle.

Sir Ron Priestley is undoubtedly interesting for the coming season, having produced two efforts full of promise in 2018, when chasing home the subsequent Group

1-placed Fox Tal on his debut at Ffos Las, before finishing fourth behind three next-time-out winners—including Godolphin's Breeders' Cup Juvenile Turf winner Line of Duty—at Goodwood in September. By Australia and out of a 103-rated mare who stayed a mile and a half, Sir Ron Priestley will be even better once tackling middle-distances this season and looks well capable of winning a novice/maiden before he heads into decent handicaps. *Mark Johnston*

Conclusion: *Represents some strong form lines and looks just the type of slow-burner that his yard is renowned for improving steadily over time, not least when going up in trip*

Skardu   96p

3 ch.c. Shamardal (USA) – Diala (Ire) (Iffraaj)
2018 7g* Sep 28

Skardu is a city in Pakistan that can be found in a valley at the confluence of the Indus and Shigar Rivers, one that was carved by glaciation thousands of years ago. There was, however, nothing glacier-like about the William Haggas-trained colt of the same name when he made a winning racecourse debut at Newmarket in late-September; for all that odds of 33/1 that day suggest he hadn't been tearing up the gallops. Soon steadied and allowed to settle into a rhythm, he started to make ground over two furlongs out and, despite a little stumble heading into the Dip, powered home on the far rail, given just a single tap of the whip entering the final furlong. The time of the race wasn't bad by any means, and Skardu was arguably value for extra on the day, given that he was the only one of the four who pulled clear to come from the back.

It was certainly a performance that merited his high rating for a juvenile debutant and there are plenty of grounds for optimism heading into his three-year-old season; he was one of only six winning two-year-old newcomers for the William Haggas yard (from more than 60 runners) last term, and though his dam failed to build on her own juvenile promise, it will be disappointing if Skardu isn't up to listed class at least in 2019. *William Haggas*

Conclusion: *Good-bodied colt (has scope) who won his maiden in the style of an above-average prospect and should not be taken lightly if lining up in a classic trial in the spring*

Solid Stone (Ire)   89p

3 br.c. Shamardal (USA) – Landmark (USA) (Arch (USA))
2018 7s⁴ 7g² t7.1d* Nov 7

Sir Michael Stoute and Saeed Suhail have forged a successful partnership over the years, with the majority of the owner's best horses having passed through the hands of the master of Freemason Lodge at some point, including classic winners King's Best and Kris Kin, and other Group/Grade 1 winners Poet's Word and Cannock Chase. Clearly, Solid Stone has a long way to go to emulate those horses, but he made a positive impression in his own right as a two-year-old and looks sure to pay his way in 2019.

Solid Stone caught the eye when fourth on his debut in a Newbury maiden—so much so that he earnt a Timeform large 'P'—and was duly a warm order to get off the mark at Doncaster a month later. He found one too good on that occasion, but did take the expected jump forward in pulling clear of the remainder, with a next-time-out winner back in third. Again sent off at odds-on for his third start, Solid Stone got the job done in a small-field event at Newcastle, and though he only scrambled home by a neck, the steady gallop was against him and he did well to pull it out of the fire, caught flat-footed two furlongs out before hitting top gear just in time.

Overall, the feeling is that those three runs have merely scratched the surface of Solid Stone's potential. He has plenty about him physically, as you'd expect from a 360,000 guineas purchase, and is bred to really come into his own over a mile and a quarter-plus, by Shamardal and a half-brother to several winners, including the smart middle-distance pair Cameron Highland and Field of Miracles. With an opening BHA mark of just 85, Solid Stone will be of clear interest in the short-term, but he also appeals as just the type from whom his trainer will coax sustained improvement over the course of his three-year-old campaign. *Sir Michael Stoute*

Conclusion: *Did well under the circumstances to make it third-time lucky at Newcastle and should prove capable of better still when the emphasis is more on stamina (likely to stay 1¼m+); opening mark of 85 could underplay his ability by some way*

Space Blues (Ire) 102p
3 ch.c. Dubawi (Ire) – Miss Lucifer (Fr) (Noverre (USA))
2018 8.3s* Nov 7

Times have changed at Godolphin since Charlie Appleby sent out 151 winners from 663 runners in Britain in 2015, with the focus since then having shifted to quality over quantity. Admittedly, quality cannot be surmised by statistics quite so easily, but the mantelpiece at Appleby's home should tell you all that you need to know about how well that transition has gone—indeed, the Godolphin man may have to clear out some garage space if 2019 proves as successful as last season, when Masar's Epsom Derby triumph was one of 11 Group 1 wins in seven different countries.

Masar is likely to have all the major middle-distance prizes on his agenda when returning as a four-year-old, but it remains to be seen who will be tasked with attempting to give Appleby a second Derby success in as many years. Quorto and Line of Duty are the shortest-priced of his prospective runners in the ante-post betting, though time is also still on Space Blues' side as he attempts to establish himself as a classic contender.

Space Blues is certainly bred to be mixing it with the best—he is by Dubawi and out of the Group 2-winning mare Miss Lucifer, making him a half-brother to the very smart Shuruq—and there was plenty of encouragement to be taken from his debut at the back end of last season, when readily winning a soft-ground Nottingham maiden by two and three quarter lengths from another member of this year's *Fifty*, Private Secretary, who had the benefit of a previous run to his name. Space Blues only had to be pushed out under hands-and-heels to beat him, and the five lengths that they put between themselves and the third marked them both out as being above-average.

Space Blues is sure to progress as a three-year-old, with a classic trial appealing as a suitable starting point in the spring; the double-figure quotes currently on offer for Epsom could prove fanciful should that initial assignment go as well as we are anticipating. **Charlie Appleby**

Conclusion: *Created a deep impression when opening his account at the first time of asking and looks another exciting prospect for his connections, who are entitled to be harbouring classic aspirations*

 ## Stylehunter   109p

4 ch.g. Raven's Pass (USA) – Sunday Bess (Jpn) (Deep Impact (Jpn))
2018 80p: 8m² 10m² p10g* 8m⁶ 9.1m* 9m Sep 29

Along with the usual array of potential classic and Group horses in his care, John Gosden can usually be relied upon to have a strong team of older handicappers, with GM Hopkins, Royal Oath, Expresso Star and Charm School all scooping big pots in recent years. The last-named pair both ran in the colours of H.R.H. Princess Haya and, in Stylehunter, it looks as if the partnership has another one worth following.

It took Stylehunter four attempts to open his account last season, but when he did it was in some style, routing a field that included the useful Sawwaah by six lengths at Lingfield in May. He doubled his tally with another comfortable success at Goodwood in August, surging clear in the final furlong in a small-field minor event.

It's as much his defeats as his successes that mark him out as a horse of interest, though, with both of his handicap runs having come in hugely competitive affairs. He was pitched in at the deep end for his debut in that sphere when a never-nearer sixth in a typically hot Britannia at Royal Ascot, beaten only two and a half lengths by subsequent Group 2 winner Ostilio (to whom he conceded 1 lb), and was then undone by the draw in the Cambridgeshire on his final start. At Newmarket, he was one of only eight who raced on the stand-side and fared second-best of that octet behind Raising Sand, who went on to take a competitive affair at Ascot on his next start.

With his career just eight starts old, the suspicion is that what Stylehunter achieved at two and three is a springboard to greater things, rather than his limit. And, whilst he's shown that he can handle a strongly-run mile on a stiff track, both of his wins have come over further, and it's at a mile and a quarter (and possibly further) that we expect to see Stylehunter flourish, a BHA mark of 99 looking lenient on what he's achieved, let alone what can be expected of him in 2019. **John Gosden**

Conclusion: *Showed an aptitude for big-field handicaps in 2018 and is fancied to find a similar event coming his way this time round, with the prospect of more to come after only eight starts*

Pat Jupp, Senior Horse Racing Analyst (Stylehunter):
"Unexposed four-year-olds are often thin on the ground in high-end handicaps, making them of above-average interest when they come along, and Stylehunter certainly fits the bill. His three-year-old campaign barely scratched the surface, easy wins at Lingfield and Goodwood interspersed between good runs in the Britannia and Cambridgeshire, neither of which saw him to full effect. He'll be interesting up to a mile and a quarter and has the attributes to take a big pot or two in 2019."

Sucellus 85P

3 b.c. Dansili – Primevere (Ire) (Singspiel (Ire))
2018 t8.6s* Dec 8

Anthony Oppenheimer's vast wealth is founded on the success of De Beers, which controls around a third of global diamond production, and he is one of a diminishing number of English owner-breeders who still maintain a broodmare band of any size. Oppenheimer keeps around 30 mares at his Hascombe and Valiant studs in Newmarket, the most famous graduate of which is undoubtedly Golden Horn, who fulfilled a lifelong ambition for his owner when winning the Derby in 2015. "It's what I've wanted all my life," Oppenheimer explained afterwards. "It's the biggest race in the world and it's why I breed racehorses."

Oppenheimer came close to scaling that peak again in 2017, when Cracksman was beaten just a length into third by Wings of Eagles, and it is not beyond the realms of possibility that the owner could be at Epsom on Derby day with another leading contender in 2019, with Sucellus boasting a very similar profile to those of Golden Horn and Cracksman at the same stage of their careers.

Like that pair, Sucellus was successful on his sole racecourse appearance as a two-year-old, when beating 10 rivals on a cold December evening at Wolverhampton. The half-length that he won that minor event by doesn't tell the whole story, either, with the true ability of Sucellus being masked somewhat by the lack of pace in the race and his own greenness through the early stages (slowly away and soon under pressure). It was only well inside the final furlong that he found top gear, and that he could win at all from his position—especially given the slow early gallop—marks him out as a useful prospect.

The large 'P' attached to his rating denotes that he should also make significant improvement at three, when he is sure to be suited by middle-distances—he saw the extended-mile out well on his debut and is certainly bred to stay (by Dansili, who is largely a stamina influence, and out of a listed winner over a mile and a quarter).

He could well have a Derby trial on his agenda in the spring, and it would certainly be unwise to read too much into the fact that he doesn't hold an entry for the premier classic at this stage; Cracksman had to be added to the Derby at a cost of £9,000 in the April of his three-year-old season, while Golden Horn was supplemented for £75,000 just five days before his historic success! *John Gosden*

Conclusion: *Looked a pattern horse in the making when winning on debut, one who is sure to win more races as a three-year-old; likely to stay 1¼m+ on breeding*

Adam Houghton, Content Editor (Sucellus):

"In 25 years on this planet, I've had the opportunity to see few better horses in the flesh than Cracksman and Golden Horn. Whether I'll be holding the same connections' Sucellus in quite so high esteem by the end of this campaign is perhaps doubtful, but I'll certainly be making the effort to clap eyes on him sooner rather than later, such was the impression he made on his debut at Wolverhampton; the way he finished his race that day marked him out as something out of the ordinary, and I expect him to take the first step towards filling some pretty big shoes in a Derby trial come the spring."

 Tabdeed   **115p**

4 ch.c. Havana Gold (Ire) – Puzzled (Ire) (Peintre Celebre (USA))
2018 6.1m* 7m 6m* Oct 5

Tabdeed's entry in the July Cup might have seemed rather fanciful after his first crack in pattern company led to a mere mid-field finish in the Jersey Stakes at Royal Ascot. His second visit to that track, however, ought to have changed the opinion of anyone still harbouring doubts.

Sent off a heavily-backed 6/4-shot to beat 10 other three-year-olds of above-average ability, Tabdeed announced himself as a youngster of high-class potential with a devastating turn of foot that enabled him to come from rear to lead inside the final furlong, even then by no means hard ridden as he opened a length advantage at the line.

That isn't Tabdeed's only piece of eye-catching form, either; in landing a Leicester minor event on his only start as a juvenile, he'd taken care of both Yafta (Group 3 winner in 2018) and Amandine (flourished into a very smart dual winner in US).

Tabdeed is bred to stay at least a mile, from the family of Derby runner-up Walk In The Park after all, but the speed he's shown so far suggests firmly that he's a natural sprinter, one very much for the notebook—and for ante-post interest in all the high-end races—in 2019. *Owen Burrows*

Conclusion: *Lightly-raced four-year-old who is in excellent hands and possesses all the tools to make a successful transition to pattern sprints in 2019*

Too Darn Hot ★   127p
3 b.c. Dubawi (Ire) – Dar Re Mi (Singspiel (Ire))
2018 8d* 7d* 7g* 7m* Oct 13

"Now, dear reader, not one of you needed to fork out £7.95 to be told that Frankel is going to be one to follow in 2011, THE one to follow in fact, and we can only hope you don't feel short-changed. Still, at the very least it's well worth detailing just what a monster he was at two and how he's going to go about pulling further clear of his contemporaries this season."

So began the entry on Frankel in the 2011 edition of *Horses To Follow*, an introduction that bears repeating in this instance because very similar sentiments apply to last season's champion two-year-old Too Darn Hot—bar the fact that this publication now costs £9.95 (blame Brexit).

Like Frankel, Too Darn Hot looked champion two-year-old material from day one, winning his maiden over a mile at Sandown in August by seven lengths, before returning to that venue the following month for the seven-furlong Solario Stakes, where he emulated Gosden's previous winners Raven's Pass and Kingman (both of whom proved top-class at three) with a four-length success, visually impressive in doing so, as well as being backed up by a smart performance on the clock.

An equally dominant winner of the Champagne Stakes at Doncaster two weeks later, Too Darn Hot secured his position at the top of the two-year-old rankings—and at the head of the ante-post Guineas market (generally 5/4)—with an authoritative performance in what was a strong renewal of the Dewhurst Stakes on his final start at Newmarket. Admittedly, he briefly looked in trouble running into the dip, but it did not take him long to find top gear once hitting the rising ground, forging clear to beat the

Too Darn Hot (pink) caps an unbeaten two-year-old season with victory in the Dewhurst

Phoenix Stakes winner Advertise by two and three quarter lengths, with the National Stakes runner-up Anthony Van Dyck another length and a quarter back in third.

Too Darn Hot has already broken the family mould by showing so much speed and precocity—his dam Dar Re Mi and full sisters So Mi Dar and Lah Ti Dar have all excelled over middle-distances—and he looks sure to take all the beating in the Guineas, before potentially putting his own stamina to the test in the Derby. Whatever his optimum trip proves to be, though, he clearly possesses vast talent and probably hasn't shown all that he is capable of yet, a tantalising thought that makes him 'THE' one to follow in 2019. *John Gosden*

Conclusion: *Most exciting prospect with a rating already in advance of the standard required to win a typical renewal of the 2000 Guineas, fully deserving of his position as short-priced favourite*

Turjomaan (USA) ★ 97p

3 b. or br.c. War Front (USA) – Almoutezah (USA) (Storm Cat (USA))
2018 7m*d t7.1s* Oct 23

Newcastle's tapeta surface, set over a straight mile which climbs uphill significantly towards the finish, provides a stiff examination of stamina under normal circumstances, but it was even more of a test on Tuesday the 23rd of October 2018, with a strong headwind ensuring some particularly slow finishes on the straight course and giving hold-up horses a big advantage, even in the more steadily-run races. On an eight-race card, seven winners came from off the pace, the only exception being the seven-furlong novice won by Turjomaan, who took up the running soon after the start and quickened off the front to readily beat his market rival Wiretap (who'd shown fairly useful form when second in a good-looking maiden at Yarmouth) by two and a half lengths. As well as bearing the brunt of the wind, Turjomaan was also conceding a penalty to Wiretap for his victory in a novice at Ascot in September, though in rather unusual circumstances; he was subsequently found to be ineligible to run in that particular race and disqualified, trainer Roger Varian receiving a fine for breaching rule (C)37.1, which states: "a trainer must ensure that he does not declare or run a horse in any race for which it is not qualified". Though he's no longer officially two-from-two, Turjomaan looks a cracking three-year-old prospect, possessing an imposing frame which is likely to see him get better and better with time, particularly when he tackles a mile (powerful galloper whose dam is closely related to a US Grade 1 winner over a mile and a quarter). **Roger Varian**

Conclusion: *Created an excellent impression in two juvenile starts and has the physique to be significantly better this season over 1m+; a potential group horse*

Ben Fearnley, Content Editor (Turjomaan):
"Roger Varian's two-year-olds were generally slow burners in 2018, so Turjomaan marked himself down as something out of the ordinary when defying big odds on debut at Ascot in September, despite looking very raw. His big price that day was certainly not down to a lack of reputation at home and, built to be significantly better as a three-year-old, I expect him to develop into a group performer this season."

Wise Counsel ★ 94p

3 b.c. Invincible Spirit (Ire) – Noozhah (Singspiel (Ire))
2018 6.5m⁶ 6m⁴ 6g³ 6g* Sep 28

Group 1 winners Harry Angel, Profitable, Lethal Force and Gilt Edge Girl are all evidence of Clive Cox's prowess with sprinters and, while it might be optimistic to expect Wise Counsel to scale the same heights as those illustrious predecessors, he looks well up to winning handicaps in 2019, with a graduation to something a bit better not out of the question should things go well.

Wise Counsel took four goes to get off the mark last season, but he had some very strong form to his name along the way, his unlucky-looking third behind San Donato (a fellow member of the *Fifty* and now rated 115p) and Hello Youmzain (rated 112p following a Group 2 win in France) at Haydock in September reading especially well, and he wasn't all out when landing the odds at the same track later that month, recording an impressive timefigure in the process. An opening handicap mark of 87 is lenient judged on either of those efforts, and Wise Counsel's good-topped physique and smart pedigree (he's a half-brother to the Group 1-placed Noozhoh Canarias) point to further improvement in the pipeline. He's raced around six furlongs so far, and while there's some stamina in his pedigree to suggest he may stay a bit further, speed has looked Wise Counsel's main asset to date. **Clive Cox**

Conclusion: *Pacey sort who reached a borderline useful standard in four runs as a juvenile and looks the type to win some good sprint handicaps, with a lenient opening mark to exploit*

Young Rascal (Fr) ★ 125p

4 b.c. Intello (Ger) – Rock My Soul (Ire) (Clodovil (Ire))
2018 11d* 12.3g* 12g 11s* 12g* Oct 27

"He ran a good race at Nottingham behind another of mine called My Lord And Master, who bolted up. Young Rascal was terribly green, he was all over the shop—on the outside then on the inside—but he did run on well, and Joe Fanning who rode him rather liked him. We put him away after that and he could just develop into a nice horse, though he's still a bit raw and may well need a race or two to get into the swing of things."

As dark horses go, Young Rascal—put forward by his trainer William Haggas in the 'Talking To The Trainers' section of *Horses To Follow 2018*—must be one of the best ever, the colt beginning his three-year-old campaign Timeform rated just 83p and ending up a whopping 125p, having won four of his five starts, with his only defeat coming in the Derby at Epsom. After shedding his maiden tag in a big field at Newbury in April, Young Rascal was quickly upped in grade and overcame trouble in running to

Young Rascal could yet develop into a top-level performer

win the Chester Vase with a bit up his sleeve, continuing a pattern of rapid progression from run to run. Unfortunately for Haggas—and particularly his owner Bernard Kantor, long-time managing director of the Derby's current sponsor Investec—Young Rascal underperformed in the Derby next time, the race perhaps coming too soon after the two big performances he had kicked the season off with. He was wisely given time to recover from this blowout and soon got back on the up, leading in the final strides of the Group 3 Legacy Cup at Newbury to beat a host of much more experienced older horses, whilst still looking far from the finished article himself.

Young Rascal had to share the spoils on his final start of the campaign in the St Simon Stakes back at Newbury, but he arguably enhanced his credentials even further, showing more pace than had been the case on his previous starts as he quickened clear of the pack two furlongs from home, rallying well when challenged but eventually joined on the line by the strong-finishing Morando. Those two battles are likely to have aided Young Rascal's development and, after just six lifetime starts, it's hard to think we've seen the best of him yet. He handles testing ground very well, though doesn't need it, and is likely to stay further than a mile and a half when required. *William Haggas*

Conclusion: *Progressed rapidly during his five three-year-old starts and wouldn't have to improve a great deal more to become a top-level performer at around 1½m this season*

Zakouski

100p

3 b.c. Shamardal (USA) – O'Giselle (Aus) (Octagonal (NZ))
2018 p7s* Nov 21

A Kempton novice event in November would hardly be the most obvious starting point when looking for a horse that could make up into a pattern performer in 2019, but Zakouski looked much better than the colts that usually turn up on all-weather at that time of year when making a winning debut. Admittedly, it wasn't a strong race overall, but it did feature Headman, another promising individual who had created a deep impression when making a winning debut of his own, so much so that he was sent off the 9/4-on favourite to follow up under a penalty. Ordinarily, Headman's performance that day would have been easily enough to see him land the odds, too, but his supporters wouldn't have counted on bumping into one with the talent of Zakouski, who immediately ran to a useful level in registering a two-length victory, impressing on both the eye and the clock as he recorded a rapid closing sectional.

Zakouski's pedigree sends out mixed messages as to what his ideal trip may ultimately be—he is a half-brother to the smart Australian sprinter Albrecht and out of a mare who is from the family of the high-class performer up to a mile and a quarter, Lonhro— but the progeny of his sire Shamardal typically progress well, and Zakouski certainly boasts sound claims of staying at least a mile. The Charlie Appleby yard is blessed with any number of once-raced, promising types to go to war with this season, but Zakouski heads into 2019 with as much potential as any, and though an outside shout at this stage, it is certainly not out of the question that he could make up into a 2000 Guineas contender. *Charlie Appleby*

Conclusion: *Ran to a high level for a newcomer when getting the better of another very promising sort at Kempton in November; sure to progress and worth looking out for in a classic trial in the spring*

SECTION

Downdraft (Ire) 106

4 b.c. Camelot – Cinnamon Rose (USA) (Trempolino (USA))
2018 p7g* p8s² 10g* 12m⁶ 11.9g⁶ 8.2d⁵ 10g 10d* Oct 21

In May 2009, Joseph O'Brien kickstarted an illustrious (if relatively brief) riding career with a first win aboard Johann Zoffany at Leopardstown, that success coming only five days after his 16th birthday. Most people at that age don't have the slightest clue what they want to do with their lives (not me—Timeform has always been my calling), but then, Joseph O'Brien has never been like 'most people' has he? The youngest jockey ever to win a race at the Breeders' Cup. The winner of 126 races on the Flat in Ireland in 2013, breaking Mick Kinane's 20-year-old record. Half of the first father and son partnership to win the Derby at Epsom.

The records have continued to tumble—both on the Flat and over jumps—since O'Brien switched his attentions to training in 2016. Given the historic nature of the race, his most notable achievement arguably came when becoming the youngest trainer to win the Melbourne Cup, courtesy of Rekindling in 2017 (when aged 24), and it is not beyond the realms of possibility that O'Brien could field another leading contender for the 2019 renewal of the 'race that stops a nation'.

Admittedly, Downdraft is yet to race beyond a mile and a half, but there is encouragement to be taken from his pedigree; he is by Camelot after all, who has so far proved a stamina influence at stud. And, with his form having plateaued slightly after scoring at Navan last June, Downdraft showed enough to suggest that he has the class to head to Flemington when resuming winning ways on his final 2018 start at Naas. Indeed, he did especially well to win that day having been held up in a slowly-run race, staying on strongly at the death to defy a mark of 93 (useful form).

The reason for suggesting that the Melbourne Cup could be his long-term aim is because he is owned by the Australian-based OTI Racing, who have made it their M.O. to acquire potential contenders for the race in recent years, only narrowly missing out with Bauer in 2008. Downdraft himself was only purchased by them last April, and, having laid the foundations in the second half of that season, he is fancied to reward them handsomely in 2019. **Joseph O'Brien**

Conclusion: *Signed off with a career best at Naas in October and has the tools to be competitive in listed/minor pattern events on that evidence, before a potential tilt at the Melbourne Cup*

facebook.com/timeform1948

Echo Park (Ire) 100p

4 br.f Elusive Pimpernel (USA) – Pershaan (Ire) (Darshaan))
2018 p7s 10m^3 9.5g^2 11.2g^2 12.5g* 12d^2 p12g* Oct 19

Progression doesn't always guarantee success in racing, but the old saying goes that 'all good things come to those who wait', and that sentiment certainly rang true for the Jessica Harrington-trained Echo Park last season.

Unraced as a juvenile, Echo Park failed to get her head in front in four starts in maidens, despite progressing steadily all the time, and it wasn't until making her handicap debut at Sligo in August that she gained the victory her consistency deserved, when making all to win by five and a half lengths after travelling through matters smoothly. A 10 lb higher mark made life tougher on her next start at the Curragh, but she again found another chunk of improvement, ultimately finding stablemate Rovetta too strong at the finish, but still proving herself to be miles ahead of her mark in pulling nine lengths clear of the remainder. Echo Park returned to Dundalk after seven weeks off in October and didn't need to improve to get back to winning ways, sticking to her task well and appearing to have more in hand than the winning margin would suggest. That form has worked out well, too, with the runner-up going on to win twice subsequently, latterly from a mark 9 lb higher than when chasing Echo Park home.

For her part, Echo Park has the scope to make an even better four-year-old, with only seven outings under her belt, and it would be no surprise if she proved better than a handicapper. Yet to race beyond a mile and a half, she will stay further on breeding (dam stayed two miles) and is one to follow this coming season. *Jessica Harrington*

Conclusion: *Came a long way in a short space of time in 2018 and remains with potential as a four-year-old; should prove capable of mixing it in listed/minor pattern company against her own sex*

Japan 113p

3 b.c. Galileo (Ire) – Shastye (Ire) (Danehill (USA))
2018 8d 7s* 8g* Sep 30

Shastye is undoubtedly one of the jewels amongst Newsells Park Stud's broodmare brand. Having already produced Secret Gesture, second in the 2013 Oaks, her last three colts have fetched 3.6m guineas, 1.3m guineas and 3.4m guineas, respectively, at Book 1 of the Tattersalls October Yearling Sale, all of them purchased on behalf of the Coolmore partners. Japan was the name given to the second of those big-money purchases, and he could well prove to be the best of the family so far on the evidence of his highly promising juvenile season.

The word 'season' is used rather loosely in this instance, when you consider that Japan's three runs all came in the month of September, a measure of the giant strides he made that he went from finishing seventh in a Curragh maiden in the first of them to winning the Group 2 Beresford Stakes in the third, with a ready success in a Listowel maiden sandwiched in between. The outsider of three Aidan O'Brien runners in the Beresford according to the betting, he produced a strong surge to nail his seemingly better-fancied stablemate Mount Everest late on, the way that the pair of them opened up a three-length gap back to the field in the final furlong suggesting that both are very promising colts, with the fact that Japan was able to concede a start (and experience) to the runner-up particularly encouraging.

The Beresford has a rich history when it comes to producing potential classic contenders over the years—Irish Derby/St Leger winner Capri and 2000 Guineas hero Saxon Warrior feature amongst O'Brien's recent winners of the race—and Japan looks as promising as any of them at this stage of his career. With middle-distances sure to bring about further improvement in him at three, it would come as no surprise if Japan emerges as one of the main players in the Ballydoyle team for Epsom, and we're hopeful that any future offspring of Shastye to go through the sales ring will be doing so as a half-sibling to a Derby winner. **Aidan O'Brien**

Conclusion: *Beautifully-bred colt who made giant strides in an abridged juvenile campaign and is one to look out for in a Derby trial in the spring (well worth a bet at 20/1 for the premier classic)*

Billy Nash, Senior Horse Racing Analyst (Japan):
"Say kon'nichiwa to the 2019 Derby winner—well, that's my hope at least. Japan may not have achieved as much as the likes of Too Darn Hot, Quorto, or stable companions Anthony Van Dyck and Magna Grecia, in what was a compressed debut campaign, but I reckon we have only seen a glimpse of his enormous potential. An impeccably-bred son of Galileo, he deserves immense credit for managing to win the Bereseford less than a month on from making his debut and I'm really looking forward to seeing what he can do at a mile and a half this year. Japan—the land of the rising sun, or, in this case, the name of a rising star."

Magna Grecia (left) came a long way in a short space of time last season

Magna Grecia (Ire)   116p

3 b.c. Invincible Spirit (Ire) – Cabaret (Ire) (Galileo (Ire))
2018 7g* 8m² 8g* Oct 27

The premier race at a mile for two-year-olds, staged at Doncaster in October and first run in 1964 as the Timeform Gold Cup, underwent a sponsorship change in 2018, with Vertem taking over the reins after almost two decades of Racing Post backing. That marked just the fifth different supporter in the race's long and illustrious history, and there's been an almost unswerving consistency to the identity of the winners, too. King's Theatre's 1993 success provided the late Sir Henry Cecil with a tenth 'Timeform Gold Cup' stretched across a 25-year span, and the latest campaign saw Aidan O'Brien close the numerical gap still further, as Magna Grecia became the eighth victor from the yard since Saratoga Springs started the Ballydoyle ball rolling in 1997.

As that modern-day dominance might suggest, Magna Grecia has a good deal to live up to; a year earlier, Coolmore's subsequent 2000 Guineas winner Saxon Warrior had edged out Roaring Lion in a stirring finish, while Camelot won the 2011 renewal. The following season his bid for the Triple Crown ended at the final hurdle back at

Doncaster in the St Leger, his second to Encke there ensuring the long wait to emulate Oh So Sharp's historic 1985 campaign was extended still further.

Magna Grecia's performance rating of 116 wouldn't have him up with the best winners of the race this century but, as the Timeform report on the race noted at the time, this was an instance "where the end-of-year rating doesn't adequately tell his story, (Magna Grecia) squeezing into a month what few two-year-olds manage in an entire season".

And that really is the kernel of the story with the thrice-raced Magna Grecia, one of only nine first-time-out juvenile winners of the year for his all-conquering yard—he's still an open book, and in precisely the right hands to fulfil his immense potential as he embarks on a three-year-old campaign that ought to bring with it more top-level success. Magna Grecia is out of a Galileo mare who contested the Oaks, but the progeny of his sire, Invincible Spirit, have tended to be best up to a mile, and Magna Grecia looks more in the latter mould himself. *Aidan O'Brien*

Conclusion: *Signs of brilliance in a mere month-long juvenile career, whetting the appetite for what may be to come once his master trainer has had more time to develop him*

Rocky Blue (Ire)   81

4 ch.g Society Rock (Ire) – Plumbago Blue (Manduro (Ger))
2018 p8s p7s 8g 10m 12g² 12.7d² 12.5g² 14g* Sep 8

The dual Group 1-winning sprinter Society Rock sadly died of laminitis just a couple of years into his stud career, having made a very promising start with his first two crops, siring the pair of Group 1 juvenile performers Unfortunately and The Mackem Bullet. Rocky Blue clearly didn't inherit such precocity, finishing well held when starting out in maidens over seven furlongs and a mile in the first half of 2018, but he improved with every run once stepped into handicaps over longer trips, second in the first three of them before annihilating the opposition when upped further in trip to a mile and three quarters at Navan.

Sent hurdling after that, he showed definite aptitude when second to Got Trumped at Punchestown first-time-out, before springing a surprise when landing the Grade 2 Knight Frank Juvenile Hurdle at Leopardstown over Christmas. Admittedly, the race was rather muddling, the time around five seconds slower than both the preceding maiden hurdles on the card, but he had to make his ground out very wide around the home turn, got to the front on the bridle early in the straight, and for all that Coeur Sublime looked the more likely winner when crashing out at the last, it still represented a significant step forward from Rocky Blue, who went on to win by three and a quarter lengths.

Unfortunately, injury ruled him out of the Spring Juvenile Hurdle in early February, and for the rest of the jumps season, but, given his hurdling exploits, he's a potentially well-handicapped horse from a current mark of 74 back on the Flat. Indeed, he's still very much unexposed at staying trips on the level, and it's easy to see him picking up a race or two from that sort of rating before presumably returning to hurdling in the autumn. **Thomas Mullins**

Conclusion: *Relished the longer trip when forging clear on his final Flat start and remains potentially well treated judged on his subsequent hurdling exploits, with 2m+ still to explore*

Skitter Scatter   113p

3 b.f Scat Daddy (USA) – Dane Street (USA) (Street Cry (Ire))
2018 p5s³ p5s* 6g³ 6m² 7.1d* 7d* 7g* Sep16

The Prendergast name was back on the roll of honour of one of Ireland's top two-year-old races in the latest season, with Patrick Prendergast becoming the third member of the famous Irish racing dynasty to win the Moyglare Stud Stakes courtesy of Skitter Scatter. He was following in the footsteps of his uncle Kevin, who has won the race on

Skitter Scatter stays on strongly to record a first Group 1 success in the Moyglare

four occasions since 1973, and his grandfather and namesake Paddy Prendergast, who won the race twice in his long and successful training career, one which also yielded 17 classic wins in Ireland and four in Britain (won all but the Derby once). Skitter Scatter's connections are bound to have classic aspirations of their own in 2019, with the 1000 Guineas likely to be first on her agenda, though it will not be Patrick Prendergast's name that appears on the roll of honour if she is successful at Newmarket—it was announced in January that he would be merging his team with that of John Oxx ahead of the new turf Flat season, with Oxx becoming the named trainer after Prendergast chose not to renew his licence at the end of February.

As surprising a development as that was, it is unlikely to have any significant bearing on Skitter Scatter's prospects for the season ahead, and she deserves to be considered a leading Guineas contender on the back of a most productive juvenile campaign. Admittedly, her first four starts didn't immediately mark her out as top two-year-old material—she recorded her only win in a Dundalk maiden in April—but she had shown herself to be a useful filly with the possibility of better still to come when stepping up to seven furlongs, and that certainly proved to be the case in the second half of the season. Wins in the Silver Flash Stakes at Leopardstown and Debutante Stakes at the Curragh, both in July, identified her as a filly on the up, and there was no more popular result on Irish Champions Weekend than her Moyglare success, when staying on strongly to provide Prendergast and jockey Ronan Whelan with their first Group 1 wins.

Skitter Scatter was ridden more patiently than has often been the case on that occasion, which offers encouragement with going up to a mile this season in mind. A likeable filly with a good attitude, it is very hard to pick holes in her, and even more difficult to see her not playing a leading role come the first weekend in May. **John Oxx**

Conclusion: *Has some of the best juvenile form in the book and makes plenty of appeal at 14/1 in an open renewal of the 1000 Guineas, with further improvement likely to be forthcoming*

Trethias 98

3 b.f Invincible Spirit (Ire) – Evita (Selkirk (USA))
2018 7g^4 8d* 7m^4 7g^4 Sep 30

"We asked 100 people to name a successful dual-purpose horse racing trainer..."

This wouldn't be the most obscure question ever posed to contestants on a poll-based television quiz show such as Pointless, or Family Fortunes back in the day, but we would be struggling to come up with a better current answer than Jessica Harrington, who last season guided Alpha Centauri to multiple Group 1 success hot on the heels of Sizing John's 2017 Cheltenham Gold Cup victory.

Trethias is starting her three-year-old campaign some way behind where Alpha Centauri was 12 months ago and seems unlikely to be following in the immediate footsteps of her former stable companion—who sadly suffered a career-ending injury when beaten by Laurens in the Matron Stakes last September—by winning the Irish 1000 Guineas, but we do think Trethias, a €400,000 purchase as a yearling, will pay her way in less exalted company in 2019.

Trethias won a Curragh maiden on just her second start as a juvenile and her only one over a mile—a trip that is likely to prove a minimum this season—with the choicely-bred next-time-out winner Pink Dogwood two and three quarter lengths back in second. Things didn't go to plan when up in grade/down in trip for her two subsequent starts, left with impossible tasks in a listed race at Leopardstown on Irish Champions Weekend and a Group 3 at Naas later in September, sent off as second favourite behind the winner Hermosa on the latter occasion.

Trethias boasts an appealing pedigree with the coming season in mind. She's a year-younger half-sister to the smart Argentello, whose form took off for John Gosden in 2018, winning four of his final six starts, and her dam Evita is closely related to the top-class middle-distance performer Rewilding and a daughter of the 1986 Prix Vermeille heroine Darara, who ended that year as Timeform's joint-top rated three-year-old filly in Europe. *Jessica Harrington*

Conclusion: *Showed useful form at two, most notably when winning her maiden over 1m, and will benefit from a return to that trip, with 1¼m likely to prove well within her range, too*

Western Frontier (USA)   94p
3 b.c Scat Daddy (USA) – Missamerica Bertie (USA) (Quiet American (USA))
2018 5.8g³ 5.8d² 5g* Oct 24

It's now over three years since the untimely death of stallion Scat Daddy, a loss that was felt more keenly than ever in 2018, with the US Triple Crown winner Justify amongst those who added their names to a growing list of star progeny, one that already included the likes of Lady Aurelia and Caravaggio. Scat Daddy is inevitably going to prove hugely difficult to replace at Coolmore, but the early signs are that he is going to prove an above-average sire of sires—his son No Nay Never was crowned champion first-season sire in 2018, after all—and work is well underway when it comes to further cementing the Scat Daddy sire-line, with Justify, Mendelssohn and Sioux Nation all having joined the Coolmore stallion ranks at the end of last season.

Western Frontier has a lot of work to do if he is going to head the same way at the end of 2019, but he's clearly a Scat Daddy colt going the right way, one who should have plenty more to offer in the coming season. Western Frontier ran three times in the space of 25 days near the back end of last term (all at Navan), running to a similar level on the first two occasions before taking a big step forward when getting off the mark in late-October, still showing signs of greenness under pressure (carried his head awkwardly) as he was driven clear in the closing stages. Western Frontier is far from the finished article physically, either, and he looks the type to go on improving throughout his three-year-old campaign, not short on speed but likely to get six furlongs and further when the time comes. ***Aidan O'Brien***

Conclusion: *Opened his account at the third attempt last season, despite still looking green, and hard to think he won't have plenty more to offer at sprint trips*

Winner Takes Itall (Fr) 89p

4 b.g Nathaniel (Ire) – Sinndiya (Ire) (Pharly (Fr))
2018 8m³ 12m⁴ Jul 21

This year will be the 45th anniversary of the Eurovision Song Contest that changed the lives of a four-piece Swedish act called Abba, who disbanded more than eight years later after having become one of the most commercially successful groups in the history of pop music. There was much fanfare when it was announced that they would be recording new material in 2019, though racing had maintained a link to

Winner Takes Itall looks a good prospect for Joseph O'Brien this season

the group for much of the intervening period thanks to Benny Andersson, who has enjoyed plenty of success as owner-breeder, perhaps most notably with the John Dunlop-trained Beatrice Aurore, a winner at Group 3 level in 2011.

The Winner Takes It All—co-written by Andersson and fellow band member Bjorn Ulvaeus—was one of Abba's biggest hits, recorded in 1980 during a period when the professional and personal relationships within the group were heading towards their own versions of 'Waterloo'. In contrast, the current partnership between owner J. P. McManus and trainer Joseph O'Brien continues to go from strength to strength, especially in the National Hunt code, and it is fair to assume that we've yet to see what the equine Winner Takes Itall is capable of, initially on the level, having not been seen to anything like best effect in a couple of maidens at the Curragh during last year's long, hot summer.

Unraced at two, Winner Takes Itall looked an unlucky loser on his belated debut in June, flashing home inside the final furlong to snatch third having encountered a troubled passage from mid-field, and he travelled like the best horse over a mile and a half three weeks later, seemingly lacking for stamina, though he hadn't done himself any favours by taking a long time to settle, either.

Either way, it may be that a mile and a quarter proves to be Winner Takes Itall's optimum trip, and this late-developer has the look of one who should improve further with time. He is certainly in the right hands to do so, and, with a maiden likely to prove a formality in the first half of the campaign, it would be no surprise if he was capable of contesting something a good deal better further down the line. *Joseph O'Brien*

Conclusion: *Offered plenty to work on amidst greenness in two starts at three and remains with potential as he gains in experience*

Yonkers (USA)   89p
3 b.c Medaglia d'Oro (USA) – Anne of Kiev (Ire) (Oasis Dream)
2018 7g^6 8.1g^2 8g^2 Aug 25

There are few more picturesque venues to watch horse racing than Killarney, and those fortunate enough to be in that part of County Kerry last July might well have been watching a couple of future classic winners. too. Joseph O'Brien's Iridessa, an impressive scorer on debut at the five-day festival, spent the winter as ante-post favourite for the Oaks after landing the Fillies' Mile at Newmarket in October, whilst 48 hours earlier Anthony Van Dyke—who ended the season as Timeform's highest-rated two-year-old trained in Ireland—had got off the mark at the second attempt before successfully stepping up into group company.

The latter's nearest rival that day was Yonkers, who like the winner was improving on the form he had shown on his debut—Yonkers must have been showing a fair bit at home prior to that 13-runner heat at Gowran Park, given that he was sent off the 6/4-favourite when finishing in mid-field. Yonkers made further improvement on his third and final outing as a juvenile, again somewhat unfortunate to bump into another above-average Aidan O'Brien-trained colt, with his victor Mount Everest subsequently just touched off by Japan (featured earlier in this section) in the Beresford Stakes.

With solid foundations already laid, a run-of-the-mill maiden is surely Yonkers' for the taking, and he looks the type to do really well in handicaps thereafter, especially when stepped up in trip; there is certainly enough in his pedigree to suggest that he'll be suited by a mile and a quarter at the very least, with his half-sister Anneli being a winner in France at that trip. An Irish Derby entry may ultimately prove fanciful, but there are certainly races to be won with Yonkers in 2019 and we'll be keen followers of his progress. **Ger Lyons**

Conclusion: *Improved with racing at two and looks a sure-fire maiden winner before graduating to pattern company/valuable handicaps in 2019; likely to stay 1¼m*

SECTION

TALKING TO THE TRAINERS

To give some pointers for the new season, we asked a number of leading Flat trainers to pick out a star performer, handicapper and dark horse to follow from their respective stables. Read on to find out which names came back...

Charlie Appleby

Wins-Runs in Britain in 2018	**88-313**
Highest-rated horse in training	**Blue Point** Timeform Rating 129

Star Performer: Quorto (122p) "This horse is very similar to his sire (Dubawi) in stature and emulated him when winning the National Stakes. He has physically done well over the winter. It looks as though a mile will be his trip and the plan is to take him straight to the 2000 Guineas at Newmarket."

Handicapper: Auxerre (110p) "A lightly-raced four-year-old who has developed well from three to four. A mile looks to be his optimum trip and he is quite versatile having won on both turf and the all-weather. The plan is to head for the Lincoln at Doncaster."

Dark Horse: Moonlight Spirit (93p) "A big, scopey horse who has done well from two to three and should further develop through his three-year-old career. Staying looks to be his forte."

Ralph Beckett

Wins-Runs in Britain in 2018	**88-522**
Highest-rated horse in training	**Air Pilot/Mount Moriah** Timeform Rating 118

Star Performer: Manuela de Vega (98p) "It was a good effort to beat the colts on only her second start in the Silver Tankard Stakes at Pontefract (useful form)."

Handicapper: Rock Eagle (107p) "He put up a smart performance when winning the Old Rowley Cup at Newmarket and we think he should progress further when going up in trip."

Dark Horse: Rowland Ward (75p) "He ran well in two starts as a two-year-old and his pedigree (by Sea The Stars and out of a half-sister to Irish Derby winner Treasure Beach) suggests that he can only get better."

Michael Bell

Wins-Runs in Britain in 2018	**56-379**
Highest-rated horse in training	**Fabricate** Timeform Rating 117

Star Performer: Pretty Pollyanna (116) "She certainly gives the impression that she has trained on. It is the intention to start in a Guineas trial at Newbury or Newmarket and how she fares will determine how her season is mapped out. I am hopeful that she will get a mile."

Handicapper: Artarmon (94) "He enjoyed a productive 2018 and, hopefully given his physique, he can make more progress this season and be competitive in the principal staying handicaps. He enjoys decent ground."

Dark Horse: Eagles By Day (81p) "He is a well bred son of Sea the Stars, who made a very promising debut at Nottingham and was put away thereafter. He has made excellent development from two to three and I am hopeful he will make up into decent staying three-year-old who will ply his trade in good company."

Saeed Bin Suroor

Wins-Runs in Britain in 2018	**84-384**
Highest-rated horse in training	**Benbatl** Timeform Rating 129

Star Performer: Dream Castle (122) "A very talented individual who has taken time to settle into racing and learn to relax. He has been gelded and is now fulfilling his full potential."

Handicapper: Team Talk (115) "A consistent type who hasn't got many miles on the clock for a six-year-old. The big handicaps at the more prestigious meetings of 2019 will be his targets."

Dark Horse: Light And Dark (81) "A nice type who is still a maiden. He was big and gangly last year, but has matured nicely over the winter and is one to watch."

Marco Botti

Wins-Runs in Britain in 2018	**34-373**
Highest-rated horse in training	**Crowned Eagle** Timeform Rating 116

Star Performer: Crowned Eagle (116) "We would have to choose him based on his form last year. He is extremely consistent and we are hoping he will pick up a nice race this year."

Handicapper: Dark Miracle (69) "He just needs one more run to be handicapped and is showing enough at home to suggest he should be an exciting prospect for this season."

Dark Horse: Lucipherus (70) "He has had three starts and finished fourth in a good maiden at Wolverhampton on the last of them. He has now been gelded and it looks like there could be plenty more to come from him."

Karl Burke

Wins-Runs in Britain in 2018	**70-634**
Highest-rated horse in training	**Laurens** Timeform Rating 120

Star Performer: Laurens (120) "A five-time Group 1 winner, she has wintered really well and, while it will not be easy for her this summer, we feel she was not given the credit she deserved last year and think there is still more to come. Her first target will be the Lockinge at Newbury."

Handicapper: Double Reflection (89) "She had a great season during 2018. She was very consistent and, while it may appear she is high in the handicap, we think she has strengthened so well that she can have another successful year."

Dark Horse: Serengeti Song (73) "He was a colt we really liked last year. He should have won first-time-out and I probably ran him back too quick after that. He has done very well and is one to watch."

Karl Burke will be hoping for more top-level success with Laurens this season

Henry Candy

Wins-Runs in Britain in 2018	**26-208**
Highest-rated horse in training	**Limato** Timeform Rating 122

Star Performer: Limato (122) "I still believe Limato has decent races in him. He continues to develop and mature, even at this late stage in his career, and he seems to retain all of his old enthusiasm."

Handicapper: Past Master (91) "He is a typical, late-maturing son of Mastercraftsman. Having had many physical problems in his early days, he appears to have overcome them now and is still on a potentially fair BHA mark of 82."

Dark Horse: Maiden Castle (67p) "He ran a good race first-time-out on the all-weather during the winter and has progressed since then. He will get a trip and should win races."

Mick Channon

Wins-Runs in Britain in 2018	**92-679**
Highest-rated horse in training	**Elidor** Timeform Rating 113

Star Performer: Chairmanoftheboard (96p) "He ran a disappointing race at Newbury in October last year, but has come back into training in great form, and will be trained for the 2000 Guineas at Newmarket."

Handicapper: Koeman (100) "He has been gelded over the winter and has been training very well. I think he can take a hand in all the big middle-distance handicaps."

Dark Horse: Modern Millie (72P) "She won first-time-out as a two-year-old. She has wintered very well and we will be aiming her at a classic trial."

Roger Charlton

Wins-Runs in Britain in 2017	**48-307**
Highest-rated horse in training	**Projection** Timeform rating 118

Star Performer: Headman (96p): "He is an imposing horse who made a very pleasing debut. We haven't had one with such presence for a while and, although he wasn't able to follow up under a penalty, it was back down in trip to seven furlongs against a horse who is well regarded. We think he will stay a mile and a quarter and he should be exciting."

Handicapper: Herculean (102p): "He is a horse with a lot of size and scope who we have always held in high regard. The ridiculous weather of last year was not ideal for him, but he has done well physically this winter and, hopefully, he can be the horse we always hoped he could be. He starts on a mark of 91."

Dark Horse: Red Impression (110p): "She is dark in the sense that she appeared under the lights at Kempton and deep in to the winter at Lingfield in winning her two races. She was noted by most because she broke the track record at Lingfield on the bridle. She will probably start at Chelmsford in the new three-year-old fillies' listed race over six furlongs on May 2nd."

Ed Dunlop

Wins-Runs in Britain in 2018	**29-408**
Highest-rated horse in training	**Red Verdon** Timeform Rating 118

Star Performer: Global Giant (112) "This horse progressed all the way through his three-year-old campaign last year, emerging from handicap company to finish placed in a pair of Group 3s before winning the listed Carlingford Stakes at Dundalk over a mile and a quarter in impressive fashion in October. He needs to find a few pounds of improvement over the winter to be genuinely competitive in stakes company, but he seems to have done particularly well from three to four and he looks a picture at the moment. Hopefully he can continue his development."

Handicapper: Dagueneau (86) "An improving staying three-year-old last year, he progressed from an opening BHA mark of 61 to 80 by the end of the season. Effective at a mile and three quarters to two miles, and on a range of different surfaces, he is a son of Champs Elysees, who was also the sire of my Ascot Gold Cup winner Trip To Paris. Whilst it might be stretching credulity to suggest he can continue to improve as that horse did, I do think he will provide Paisley Park's owner Andrew Gemmell with a lot of fun during the coming months nonetheless."

Dark Horse: Jabalaly (80p) "He ran just once at two, when chasing home the subsequently Group-3 placed Space Traveller at Doncaster. Unfortunately, Jabalaly suffered a season ending injury shortly afterwards, but he has come back into training in good form recently. Although his sire Moohaajim has been leased to Denmark for the current covering season, he did achieve some fairly impressive results with his limited number of first crop runners in 2018. Hopefully Jabalaly can add to the stallion's winning tally before too long."

Charlie Fellowes

Wins-Runs in Britain in 2018	**25-214**
Highest-rated horse in training	**Prince of Arran** Timeform Rating 118

Star Performer: Prince of Arran (118) "He nearly pulled off an unbelievable result when finishing third in the Melbourne Cup last year. The main aim is to head back to Australia this year, but his mid-season target in England could be something like the Hardwicke, as he has run very well around Ascot. I think a mile and a half to a mile and three quarters is his best trip."

Handicapper: Carnwennan (88) "A big late developing stayer—the sort of horse I love—he really started to get his act together at the end of last year, taking a valuable handicap at Nottingham, before doing everything but winning at Kempton. He's been given the winter off to develop again and could be a really nice stayer this year."

Dark Horse: Maid For Life (71p) "Second on her only start at Chelmsford as a two-year-old, this Nathaniel filly is bred to get better and better with age. She has done very well over the winter and I would be hopeful that she could turn into a stakes filly somewhere along the line."

William Haggas

Wins-Runs in Britain in 2018	**145-657**
Highest-rated horse in training	**Sea of Class** Timeform Rating 129

Star Performer(s): Sea of Class (129) and Ummalnar (104) "Obviously, Sea of Class is our star performer. She is fairly straightforward providing she stays fit and healthy. As far as another one goes, Ummalnar is a filly who I like a lot. She won a maiden and a novice very comfortably, but was slightly disappointing when upped in grade for a listed race in France. However, she is a half-sister to Sheikhzayedroad and very likely to stay quite a bit further. I very much hope that she'll be able to get proper black type this year. She may well start in the Dahlia Stakes at Newmarket, but I think a mile and a quarter, and maybe even further somewhere down the line, will be up her street. She has always worked like a nice filly at home."

Handicapper: Al Muffrih (102p) "He is a horse who I've always liked, though he's not been as straightforward as I'd hoped so far. However, he has had a long break now after being gelded and I think the form of his Sandown run has been enhanced several times. He did everything wrong when winning a maiden at Newbury in the spring, but battled back after looking sure to get swamped and I'm sure he will be dangerous

William Haggas has a typically strong team to go to war with in 2019

if he can settle in his races. I'd love to aim him at the Duke of Edinburgh at the Royal Meeting, as fast ground will suit him well."

Dark Horse: Sea Wings (unraced) "A full brother to Mutakayyef who was very immature last year, but he has always moved well and seems to have grown up quite a bit over the winter. He is the type who will improve considerably with racing and could make up into a very nice horse in the second half of the season."

David Menuisier

Wins-Runs in Britain in 2018	**12-125**
Highest-rated horse in training	**Thundering Blue** Timeform Rating 122

Star Performer: Danceteria (111) "It would be obvious to say Thundering Blue, but instead I will opt for Danceteria. He was a very progressive three-year-old last season, winning four races on the bounce, and is now BHA-rated 103. He always gave me the feeling he had the same profile as Thundering Blue, so hopefully he will prove me right."

Handicapper: Migration (73p) "He was a very green and backward two-year-old last year. He gives me the impression that he could well be on an upward curve this year and might improve as he gets wiser."

Dark Horse: Loch Laggan (unraced) "A well-bred son of Sea The Stars who worked in a very satisfactory manner a few times last year in the morning, but was too weak to make his debut. He is a huge, powerful horse, and I'd like to think he could be an interesting one to follow once the penny drops."

Hughie Morrison

Wins-Runs in Britain in 2018	**44-394**
Highest-rated horse in training	**Marmelo** Timeform Rating 123

Star Performer: Marmelo (123) "He has shown that he is a top-class stayer, who, given his speed over the last four furlongs of the Melbourne Cup, may be able to perform to the same level on soft ground over a mile and a half."

Handicapper(s): Quicksand (83) and Spargrove (50) "A potential staying handicapper, Quicksand is from a good staying family and will improve for a galloping track, while Spargrove is 17 hands and can only improve for distance—he is a half-brother to Marmelo and Vent de Force, both of whom stay two miles."

Dark Horse(s): Mums Hope (78p) and Telecaster (unraced) "Both Mums Hope and Telecaster could surprise! Telecaster is bred to be good and is going well, whilst Mums Hope did surprisingly well last season considering how slow she was to come to hand."

Kevin Ryan

Wins-Runs in Britain in 2018	**76-620**
Highest-rated horse in training	**Brando** Timeform Rating 123

Star Performer: Brando (123) "A stalwart of the sprinting division and, having won a Group 1 in 2017, he has been unlucky to not add to that at the top level. Two seconds last year and another win in the Abernant showed that he is as good as ever and he will be contesting all the major sprints once again. Although now seven, he is still lightly-raced for a sprinter."

Handicapper: Major Jumbo (114) "He took his form to another level last year, proving to be very consistent throughout and rounding off the campaign with a good win in the Coral Sprint at York. He looks to be getting better with age and will be aimed at all the top sprint handicaps—he may even develop into a pattern performer."

Dark Horse: Secret Venture (90p) "He made a winning debut, then had a long time off before running in the big sales race at York. He went to Ayr for a listed event and showed an electric turn of foot before the testing ground just caught him out late on. He's a lovely colt who was always going to do better with time, and could develop into a nice sprinter."

David Simcock

Wins-Runs in Britain in 2018	**57-470**
Highest-rated horse in training	**Desert Encounter** Timeform Rating 120

Star Performer: Mrs Sippy (111) "A likely improver from three to four, she is a big, imposing filly with a high cruising speed. She didn't finish her race off at Newmarket due to getting wound up going down and at the stalls. She should be seen to best effect at a mile and a half in fillies' pattern races."

Handicapper: Prejudice (88p) "New to us this year (formerly with the now-retired Luca Cumani), you would hope to see him make natural progression from two to three years. He will start off over a mile and a quarter, hopefully going through the ranks up to a mile and a half, and seems a very straightforward horse to deal with."

Dark Horse: Vexed (79p) "A three-year-old who is likely to progress throughout the season."

James Tate

Wins-Runs in Britain in 2018	**41-263**
Highest-rated horse in training	**Invincible Army/Kyllang Rock** Timeform Rating 117

Star Performer: Hey Gaman (116) "French 2,000 guineas runner-up who looks bigger and better this year. With no penalties, he can start at Listed level and move up."

Handicapper: Attainment (83p) "A huge Exceed and Excel three-year-old colt who ran well in all three of his starts last autumn, culminating in winning at Lingfield in October. He must improve this year and, hopefully, an opening BHA mark of 79 shouldn't be his ceiling."

Dark Horse: Astonished (82p) "A big, four-year-old filly by Sea The Stars who is delicate but talented. She won her only start at Kempton in December without needing a reminder and could be a black-type filly."

RISING STARS

Richard John O'Brien

Base	**Ballingarry, County Limerick**
First full licence	**2016**
First winner	**Alans Pride** Dundalk 27/01/2017
Total winners	**28**
Best Flat horse trained	**Maths Prize** Timeform Rating 107

A report by the Irish Horseracing Regulatory Board (IHRB) revealed that the total number (Flat and National Hunt) of trainers' licenses fell from 805 in 2007 to 578 in 2017, and is falling each year. The situation is arguably even more critical over jumps, where the vast majority of trainers are seriously struggling to make a living without the patronage of leading owners such as Gigginstown House Stud and J. P. McManus, but the same sentiments still apply at the top level on the Flat, with the majority of big races being won by the same few names. It is clearly a concern that the so-called 'smaller' trainers are being squeezed out, but Richard O'Brien is one man who has bucked the trend and taken significant steps forward in a relatively short space of time, operating in his words from "a small yard with ambitions to become big". O'Brien rode as an amateur in his late-teens and early-twenties with limited success—he remembers one solitary win on his website in a confined maiden point-to-point at The Pigeons—and it was as a dentist that he earned a living before taking out his trainer's licence at the end of 2016, with a five-year stint at David O'Meara's yard sandwiched in between. O'Brien refers to his time in Yorkshire as "a massive eye-opener" and he certainly seems to have applied the practices he observed there to his own operation. Like O'Meara before him, O'Brien has developed a reputation for sweetening up and reviving the fortunes of cheaply-bought horses from other yards, with few finer cases in point than Beach Bar. A six-year-old who had not won for nearly two years when arriving in Ireland in the summer of 2017, he has developed into one of the most prolific performers for his new stable, scoring four times and bouncing right back to his useful best when recording the most recent of his wins at Killarney last July. Overall, O'Brien saddled 13 winners in his first full season with a licence in 2017, including four wins for Tom Dooley and three for Alans Pride (also his trainer's first winner at Dundalk in the January of that year), both of whom were emerging from spells in the doldrums for their previous connections. It was a similar story with the best horse O'Brien has trained to date, Maths Prize, who provided his trainer with two of his 15 successes in the latest season (14 in Ireland and one in the UK), and only narrowly missed out on his final start in a listed race at Roscommon last July. He was subsequently sold to race in Hong Kong—where he goes by the name of Kungfumaster Panda—and the aim for O'Brien in 2019 will likely be to find his replacement, a horse who can take him to all the big days and help him to compete with the 'same few names' who have dominated the Irish Flat racing scene for so long.

Paddy Twomey

Base	**Cashel, County Tipperary**
First full licence	**2012**
First winner	**Hunting Goddess** Dundalk 11/04/2012
Total winners	**19**
Best Flat horse trained	**Foxtrot Liv** Timeform Rating 98

Paddy Twomey has only really dabbled in training racehorses since taking out his licence in 2012, and he is perhaps better known for his achievements across the bloodstock industry, both as a breeder and a consigner of two-year-old breeze-up horses. The Group 1 winners Serious Attitude and Tagula—who is also the sire of Canford Cliffs and Limato—feature amongst the best horses bred by Twomey, while it was probably his work as a consignor that allowed him to hone his terrific eye for a young horse, something that has been evident in his dealings with a small string of Flat horses at his Athassel House Stables. Indeed, the trainer has quickly become a force to be reckoned with in two-year-old maidens on the Flat, building up an excellent record from limited runners—many of whom have carried Twomey's own colours before being sold on, including Van der Decken. An impressive winner of a Curragh maiden on his debut in 2016, he was subsequently bought by Sheikh Mohammed and went on to become Twomey's first runner at Royal Ascot, carrying the Godolphin blue to fifth in the Coventry Stakes before being transferred to the yard of Charlie Appleby. It is not beyond the realms of possibility that Twomey could be back at the Royal meeting with more runners in 2019, a year that will see his 'dabbling' days come to an end, with the trainer having made a concerted effort during the winter to boost his ammunition. "I suppose I know plenty of people in the business and I let it be known that this year I wanted to train in a more public fashion," he revealed in an interview with Thoroughbred Daily News (TDN) in February. "I think that maybe there was a misconception that I was training for myself only." Twomey's call to arms certainly seems to have been heeded—he has assembled his biggest ever team of juveniles ahead of this season, reportedly numbering more than 30—and it would be a big surprise if he didn't surpass his career-best tally of seven winners (from only 28 runners) in 2018, with the three-year-olds Decrypt and Foxtrot Liv also appealing as a pair that could be up to contesting some good races in the months ahead. The former, who is still owned by Twomey, hasn't been seen since winning a Curragh maiden in June, but that form has worked out well—the third Lady Kaya went on to fill the runner-up spot in the Moyglare Stud Stakes—and he is reported to be back in good form after suffering from growing pains in the second half of 2018. Meanwhile, Foxtrot Liv finished second at listed and Group 3 level after winning her maiden and is likely to have a Guineas trial on her agenda in the spring, with Twomey welcoming the opportunity to continue his association with her American owner Martin Schwartz, the man of Stacelita and Zagora fame who bought Foxtrot Liv after her Curragh success.

Jason Watson

Attached stable	**Roger Charlton**
First ride	**2017**
First winner	**Many Dreams** Salisbury 18/05/2017
Total winners in Britain	**113 (to end of 2018)**
Best horse ridden	**Gifted Master** Timeform Rating 120

No jockey better fits the title of 'rising star' this year than Jason Watson, who went from riding just two winners in his first season with a licence to becoming champion apprentice a year later with a total of 111 victories in 2018. That meteoric rise has earned the 18-year-old a plum job as stable-jockey to Roger Charlton in 2019, even though Watson, who described the appointment as 'a huge surprise', had never ridden before for the Beckhampton trainer. Charlton, though, was clearly among those Watson has impressed over the last year or so, describing him as 'very strong, stylish, determined and he has a good understanding of race tactics'. While it was Gary Moore who provided Watson with his very first winner, he has Andrew Balding as the trainer to thank most for his rapid rise in 2018, following in the footsteps of other young jockeys such as David Probert, William Buick and Oisin Murphy (himself a former *Horses to Follow* 'rising star'), all former champion apprentices attached to Kingsclere. Others instrumental in the teenager's success have been his Derby-winning jockey coach John Reid and his agent Tony Hind. Watson's highest-profile success in Britain came when guiding top-weight Gifted Master to a dramatic last-stride win for Hugo Palmer

Jason Watson poses for pictures with Gifted Master after winning the Stewards' Cup

in the Stewards' Cup, but a still bigger victory came abroad when he landed the first Group 1 win of his career on God Given in the Premio Lydia Tesio at Rome, a win that will also go into the record books as the final one of Luca Cumani's training career. While no jockey in the post-war era has gone straight from winning the apprentice title to becoming senior champion a year later, Watson is as short as 10/1 to do just that and certainly has time on his side in achieving that ambition one day.

Nicola Currie

Attached stable	**Jamie Osborne**
First ride	**2013**
First winner	**Believe It** Kempton 20/12/2016
Total winners in Britain	**101 (to end of 2018)**
Best horse ridden	**Major Jumbo** Timeform Rating 114

Nicola Currie rode the second treble of her career at Chelmsford in January, coincidentally on the very same card as when first achieving the feat 12 months earlier. It's important that Currie—lady rider of the year in 2018—keeps up the pace this season, having set her sights on breaking the record for the most number of wins in a calendar year by a woman jockey, currently held by her role model Josephine Gordon on 106 (Hayley Turner is the only other woman to have broken the 100 barrier). Currie notched 81 wins in 2018 and rode out her claim at Kempton in November on Hold Still. Those sorts of totals must have seemed unlikely early in her riding career, which she initially considered abandoning, but a move from her native Scotland ('not many jockeys come from the Isle of Arran'), where she started out in show jumping and schooling over jumps for Lucinda Russell, ultimately led to her securing a job in Lambourn with Richard Hughes, who supplied her first winner, Believe It, at Kempton late in 2016. Winners started to flow in the second half of 2017, and she struck up a good relationship with the John Berry-trained gelding Kryptos, winning three races on him, including a good handicap at Doncaster on St Leger day, while an even more prolific partnership was established on the all-weather in the early months of 2018, when she won no fewer than five handicaps on Spare Parts, trained by Phil McEntee. Currie is now based with Jamie Osborne, and, just before losing her claim, his stable provided her with the biggest success of her career to date when Raising Sand won the valuable Challenge Cup at Ascot.

 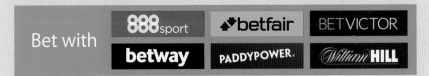

CLASSIC ANTE-POST

Timeform's Feature Writer John Ingles takes a look at the markets for the first four classics and picks out his value bets . . .

Before looking ahead to this year's races, a quick look back (through our fingers, or from behind the sofa) at some nightmarish results, from a punting point of view, in last year's classics. Billesdon Brook's form at two was 'there in the book' as the saying goes—all eight starts of it—but none of it, including a Group 3 win at Goodwood, really suggested she'd be up to winning the 1000 Guineas. But that's exactly what she did at odds of 66/1, the longest-priced of Richard Hannon's three fillies in the race. In comparison, Forever Together's Oaks win at 7/1 was much less of a surprise on the day, though again she wasn't even her stable's apparent number one contender; Aidan O'Brien's five-strong team was headed by Magic Wand, who'd beaten Forever Together in the Cheshire Oaks. A

Saxon Warrior leads home subsequent Derby winner Masar (blue) in last year's 2000 Guineas

couple of unsuccessful starts in late-season Leopardstown maidens were all ante-post punters had to go on as far as an Oaks bid was concerned, and Forever Together had still not won a race by the time she lined up at Epsom.

On the face of it, the results of the colts' classics were much more punter-friendly. Both Saxon Warrior and Masar had shown clear classic potential, both figuring among the top dozen or so colts of their crop on Timeform's two-year-old ratings. But anyone with ante-post bets on Masar for the 2000 Guineas and Saxon Warrior for the Derby can consider themselves particularly unlucky. Each started favourite for those respective classics, but, as it turned out, it was a double case of 'right horse, wrong race', with Saxon Warrior beating Masar into third at Newmarket and then 16/1 shot Masar turning the tables on the odds-on Saxon Warrior, who managed only fourth over the extra half-mile at Epsom. So, let's look at the 2019 classics…what could possibly go wrong?

2000 Guineas

Saxon Warrior was one of only two unbeaten colts in last year's Guineas, but this year's race promises to put a lot more unblemished records on the line and, as such, looks like being a contest to savour. Does that make it a harder race to weigh up? Not according to the betting, which has **Too Darn Hot** as favourite at just a shade of odds against. Some unbeaten records are more easily earned than others, but Too Darn Hot was tested more rigorously than most, and he followed impressive wins in the Solario Stakes and Champagne Stakes with one of the best Dewhurst performances seen this century when beating Phoenix Stakes winner **Advertise** and **Anthony Van Dyck**.

Three more unbeaten colts are next in the Guineas betting, though National Stakes winner **Quorto**, Middle Park Stakes winner **Ten Sovereigns** and Coventry Stakes winner **Calyx** weren't tested to quite the same extent as Too Darn Hot. His stable-companion Calyx had the excuse of an injury for not being seen after beating Advertise at Royal Ascot, while Godolphin's Quorto was put away after beating Anthony Van Dyck on that rival's home turf in the National Stakes. Ten Sovereigns moved ahead of Anthony Van Dyck in the Ballydoyle pecking order for the Guineas, though whether he has the stamina to go beyond six furlongs is questionable, with his jockey Donnacha O'Brien having described him as a 'natural sprinter'.

Madhmoon and **Royal Meeting** are further unbeaten pattern winners who might add to a potentially stellar line-up, while Vertem Futurity Trophy winner **Magna Grecia** gives Ballydoyle a contender already proven at the trip. Godolphin's hand has been strengthened by the purchase of a half-share in exciting French colt **Persian King**, who was given valuable experience of Newmarket's undulations (like other Andre Fabre-trained Guineas challengers before him) when beating Magna Grecia narrowly in the Autumn Stakes.

There's not much time once the turf season starts for late-comers to muscle their way into a Guineas picture which already looks crowded with credible rivals to Too Darn Hot. However, if the likes of **Skardu** or **Zakouski**—both members of our *Fifty*—can build on highly promising debut wins last year, maybe there'll be room to squeeze in yet another unbeaten colt in the Guineas field.

John Gosden just needs a 2000 Guineas to complete a full house of English classics, and if Too Darn Hot makes a winning return in the Greenham Stakes beforehand, he may well be odds-on to do just that.

Recommendation: **Too Darn Hot**

1000 Guineas

Such was the impression she created when winning the Breeders' Cup Juvenile Fillies' Turf in the autumn, there was inevitably a sense of disappointment when it emerged that American filly Newspaperofrecord was not amongst the 1000 Guineas entries that came through at the beginning of March, with her connections instead choosing to wait until the Coronation Stakes for her first foray overseas. Nevertheless, we should still have a good idea of where she stands in the pecking order by the time Royal Ascot comes around, with several of her victims at Churchill Downs set to line up on the Rowley Mile in her absence, including **East**, who was beaten nearly seven lengths when second in America, and **Just Wonderful**, who was another length back in fourth.

East was unbeaten in two starts for Kevin Ryan prior to that, including a Group 3 in France, and she was probably slightly better than the bare result last time, doing well under the circumstances to finish where she did from her draw (widest of all), while Just Wonderful was another who could never really get into the race after a slow start at Churchill Downs, never nearer than at the finish. She is perhaps better judged on her earlier win in the Rockfel Stakes on the Rowley Mile (readily by a length and three quarters), though even that doesn't appeal as the strongest form for the grade.

Aidan O'Brien could also rely on **Fairyland**, who had a solid record at two, signing off with wins in the Lowther Stakes and Cheveley Park. Her pedigree doesn't provide much encouragement for her staying a mile, though, a comment that also applies to stablemate **So Perfect** and the Michael Bell-trained **Pretty Pollyanna**, who finished third and fourth, respectively, in that Cheveley Park. The latter was a disappointing favourite on that occasion and seemed to find this trip a step too far when third in the Fillies' Mile on her final start, but she still ended as the season as Timeform's top-rated two-year-old filly in Britain, by virtue of her win in the Prix Morny.

The top two-year-old filly in Ireland, on the other hand, was the likeable **Skitter Scatter**, who improved all year and recorded the last of her three consecutive pattern wins for Patrick Prendergast in the Moyglare Stud Stakes, when she had a trio from

Ballydoyle (including Just Wonderful) trailing in her wake. That was a good test of stamina at the trip, and, of those towards the head of the betting, she looks to have much the strongest claims. Incidentally, if she does win the Guineas, it will be for John Oxx, whose stable has merged with that of Skitter Scatter's former handler.

Recommendation: Skitter Scatter

The Derby

Too Darn Hot is clear favourite for the Derby, as well as the 2000 Guineas, but while we're happy to take a short price about him at Newmarket, he makes less appeal at cramped odds for Epsom. He's bred to stay at least a mile and a half, but while his sister Lah Ti Dar was second in the St Leger, John Gosden reportedly sees Too Darn Hot as taking more after their sire Dubawi than their dam Dar Re Mi, who was a very smart mile and a half performer. What Too Darn Hot has already achieved at two certainly backs up the view that he's a very different animal to his later-developing sister.

As Saxon Warrior goes to show, colts like Sea The Stars and Camelot who have both the speed for the Guineas and the stamina for the Derby don't come along every year. Maybe we don't look have to look too far for an alternative to Too Darn Hot at Epsom, though, because Gosden has others who could potentially develop into live Derby

John Gosden looks to have plenty of options for this year's Derby

candidates. Foremost among those is Dubai Warrior, who looked an excellent prospect when easily justifying short odds on his only start at Chelmsford in November. Out of a smart globe-trotting mare, Mahbooba, a daughter of Galileo who won at up to a mile and a half, **Dubai Warrior** has the right sort of pedigree for the Derby but not an entry as yet, though that could be put right if he earns a wildcard place by winning the Blue Riband Trial at Epsom in April as others from his stable have done.

Quorto, by Too Darn Hot's sire Dubawi and out of a mare who finished third in the Oaks, is another with an eye on both classics, but Godolphin have another live Epsom candidate in Breeders' Cup Juvenile Turf winner **Line of Duty**. He's a son of Galileo, a sire more readily associated with providing much of Aidan O'Brien's Epsom firepower, and that looks sure to be the case again this year.

While **Anthony Van Dyck** is prominent in the Derby betting, our preference among the Ballydoyle possibles is **Japan**, who followed in Saxon Warrior's footsteps (and future St Leger winner Capri the year before) by winning the Beresford Stakes at Naas on his final start. He improved in leaps and bounds in three quick starts last September, and Japan, a brother to Oaks runner-up Secret Gesture, can continue in a similar vein over longer trips this year.

Recommendations: Dubai Warrior, Japan

The Oaks

If the 1000 Guineas picture is looking murky, then it's a sure sign that the Oaks will be no clearer. Last year's form book is only going to go some of the way to providing clues as to what might happen at Epsom on the final Friday in May, and as with the Derby, finding a potential Oaks winner at this stage is as much about seeking out promising fillies with stamina potential for a mile and a half, rather than necessarily those already proven at a high level at two. That said, **Iridessa** is a worthy favourite on both counts, having won the Fillies' Mile in the manner of a future middle-distance filly rather than a miler, as to be expected of a daughter of Derby winner Ruler of The World.

She's trained by Joseph O'Brien but, not surprisingly, his dad isn't short of likely types again, including Guineas candidate **Just Wonderful** and Fillies' Mile runner-up **Hermosa**, who looks just the sort to excel at middle-distances this term. Also worth a mention is **Chablis**, who is much more of an unknown quantity after winning a maiden at Gowran on her only start and very much bred to be suited by the Oaks trip.

Ralph Beckett has won the Oaks twice already with Look Here and Talent, and he has several fillies with classic potential in his yard this year, though telling the various daughters of Lope de Vega apart is easier said than done. **Feliciana de Vega** and **Manuela de Vega** are both unbeaten and the latter, in particular, has a pedigree that suggests this longer trip will be within range, but a darker Oaks possible in our *Fifty*

Nearooz (left) has the potential to develop into an Oaks contender

is **Dancing Vega**, who was most impressive when beating subsequent listed winner Blue Gardenia in a maiden at Doncaster.

Roger Varian also looks to have a promising batch of three-year-old fillies, and one with Oaks potential at this stage is another *Fifty* member **Nearooz**. Her debut win at Newmarket was gained narrowly, but that was over seven furlongs, and as a daughter of Derby winner New Approach (Masar's sire) out of a smart winner up to a mile and a quarter, she has plenty of scope for improvement over middle distances.

Recommendations: Dancing Vega, Nearooz

TOP ON TIME

We a pick out a few dark horses who produced notable performances on the clock in 2018…

Timefigures measure the performance of horses not on their form against one another but in terms of time, in seconds (per five furlongs) faster or slower than a certain fixed standard, and they can often be used to identify good or outstanding horses long before they can be recognised as such on form evidence, with no finer example in the latest season than **Without Parole**.

An impressive winner of his sole start at two, the timefigure (117) he recorded when reappearing in a minor event at Yarmouth last April was simply outstanding for a horse so inexperienced—only three horses have recorded a higher timefigure on their second start—and the way that he finished his race after chasing a fast pace (both contributing to his brilliant performance against the clock) marked him out as a horse who could hold his own in a higher grade. He duly went on to win the St James's Palace Stakes at Royal Ascot, when posting a higher timefigure still of 122.

Without Parole holds off the challenge of Gustav Klimt to win the St James's Palace Stakes

TOP ON TIME

Whether we can identify another Without Parole in this feature, only time will tell, but there are certainly plenty of horses who are going slightly under the radar ahead of this season, despite having caught the eye of our clock-watchers last term. **Dubai Warrior**, **Red Impression** and **Space Blues**—all members of our *Fifty*—are just three such examples, but there are plenty more who didn't quite make this year's list.

Jalmoud is one who could easily have made the cut, having impressed our sectional times analysts when second on his debut at Newcastle in November. Bred in the purple (by New Approach and out of the Oaks winner Dancing Rain), he simply needed the experience too much to play a more prominent role—he was slowly into his stride and then ran green when pushed along over two furlongs—but the ground he made up once the penny dropped, having conceded first run to the winner, was eye-catching to say the least. He looks sure to progress with that outing under his belt, and it would be no surprise to see him develop into a useful middle-distance performer this season.

Similar comments apply to the Simon Crisford-trained **Ebbraam**, who shaped well amidst greenness when third on his first start at Wolverhampton in November. Left with plenty to do as the field entered the home turn, it took him a while to start going forward in the straight, but he was ultimately finishing as well as anything and did well to snatch third close home (beaten three lengths). The form looks fair on the limited

Sheikh Hamdan looks set to enjoy a productive season

evidence so far (fourth won next-time-out) and he looks a banker for a similar event before long, with the potential to climb higher still as he gains in experience.

Sheikh Hamdan Al Maktoum is the owner of five members of the *Fifty*, and, in the shape of **Badayel** and **Jabalaly**, he appears to have two more interesting sorts to look forward to this season. The former looked unlucky not to make a successful debut at Wolverhampton in December, just failing after conceding first run, and the way he finished his race saw him receive a significant sectional upgrade, while Jabalaly was given as Ed Dunlop's 'Dark Horse' in the Talking To The Trainers section, and it is not difficult to see why. He recorded a notable timefigure for a debutant when second at Doncaster in July and should have a productive three-year-old campaign if over the problems that have kept him off the track subsequently.

The Martyn Meade-trained **Crackling** also deserves a mention, having produced a rare burst of speed to making a winning racecourse bow at Lingfield on New Year's Eve, while **Audayra** received the biggest sectional upgrade of any horse in this feature when second on her debut at Kempton in November. Sent off at 50/1, she finished with a flourish once she got the hang of things and only narrowly failed to put her head in front where it counts; the form received a boost when the third won next-time-out and she is one to watch this season with middle-distances likely to see her in an even better light.

Others to note include **Ardiente** and **Nooshin**, who both finished notably strongly when first and third, respectively, in a minor event at Kempton in November, while Joseph O'Brien's **Grandmaster Flash** appeals as one to keep onside in Ireland over the coming months. He found one too good on both his starts at Dundalk during the winter, but there was no disgrace in his second behind Playa del Puente last time, with that rival having since following up in listed company. The pair pulled a long way clear in a quick closing sectional when they met over a mile in December, and Grandmaster Flash looks sure to prove even more effective over middle-distances this term, with his Irish Derby entry suggesting that he is held in high regard.

FIRST-SEASON SIRES

Golden Horn (Highest Timeform Rating 134)

Cape Cross (Ire) – Fleche d'Or (Dubai Destination (USA))

Golden Horn was thoroughly deserving of the title of Europe's Horse of the Year in 2015, with his six wins (from eight starts) in a splendidly bold campaign including the Derby and Prix de l'Arc de Triomphe. The decision was then made to retire him at the end of his classic year, with owner Anthony Oppenheimer choosing to entrust him to Darley's Dalham Hall Stud in Newmarket, where he stood his first season in 2016 at a fee of £60,000. That immediately marked him out as one of the priciest stallions standing in Britain, but breeders were undeterred, and Golden Horn's first book of mares was unsurprisingly one of high quality—he covered 74 Group 1 winners, dams of Group 1 winners or immediate relatives of Group 1 winners. Those who chose to utilise his services were well rewarded, too, with his yearlings in 2018 selling for an average of £152,775, including a colt out of the listed winner Astonishing, who sold to BBA Ireland for 550,000 guineas, and a half-brother to the smart pair Bonfire and Joviality, who went the way of Blandford Bloodstock for 300,000 guineas. Given that Golden Horn raced just once at two, when winning a back-end maiden at Nottingham, we won't start to see the best of his first crop until the second half of 2019 (and beyond), but they are likely to prove well worth waiting for if their sire transfers even a portion of his ability.

Muhaarar (Highest Timeform Rating 134)

Oasis Dream – Tahrir (Ire) (Linamix (Fr))

Muhaarar matched Golden Horn's four Group 1 wins in 2015, sweeping all before him in the sprint division just as John Gosden's charge had over middle-distances. A Group 2-winning two-year-old, Muhaarar saved his best performance for last when beating the Sprint Cup winner Twilight Son by two lengths in the Champion Sprint Stakes, in the process surpassing even the pick of his sire Oasis Dream's efforts. Like Golden Horn, he was retired at the end of 2015 and unsurprisingly proved in high demand in his new role at owner Sheikh Hamdan Al Maktoum's Nunnery Stud, covering 129 mares in his first season. His debut yearlings sold for an average of £177,628—all from a fee of £30,000—with a high of 925,000 guineas for the half-sister to last season's Cheveley Park Stakes winner Fairyland, who, along with the 500,000 guineas colt out of multiple Group 1 winner Alexander Goldrun, will carry the silks of Sheikh Hamdan on the track, just as their sire had before them. Indeed, there has been no more loyal supporter of Muhaarar in his second career than Sheikh Hamdan, who will be hoping that he

Muhaarar was a four-time Group 1 winner over sprint trips in 2015

can prove a worthy successor to his grandsire Green Desert, and it is not difficult to envisage him challenging for leading first-season sire honours in 2019; he is by an influential sire of sires in Oasis Dream, whose son Showcasing continues to go from strength to strength, and Muhaarar should get plenty of sharp sorts if the precocity he demonstrated in his own exemplary career is anything to go by.

Free Eagle (Ire) (Highest Timeform Rating 127)
High Chaparral (Ire) – Polished Gem (Ire) (Danehill (USA))

Injury restricted Free Eagle to only four combined starts on the track at two and three, but Dermot Weld's charge was a horse who attracted plenty of headlines all the way through his career—he was promoted to Derby favouritism after making a winning debut as a juvenile—and he belatedly showed himself to be a high-class performer when returning in the autumn of his classic year, winning a Group 3 at Leopardstown by nine lengths, before finishing a creditable third behind Noble Mission and Al Kazeem in the Champion Stakes. His four-year-old campaign yielded a deserved first Group 1 success in the Prince of Wales's Stakes and a good third behind Golden Horn in the Irish Champion Stakes (when hampered by that rival), performances that saw him command a fee of €20,000 when retiring to the Irish National Stud at the end of that season. There were several six-figure lots amongst his first yearlings to change hands in 2018, including a half-brother to the dual Group 3-winning Yellow Rosebud, who sold to Shadwell for €400,000, and a half-sister to the smart pair Daban and Thikriyaat, who was bought by Charlie Gordon Watson for 250,000 guineas. With his best performances having come at middle-distances, the compact Free Eagle is unlikely to be the fastest out of the blocks with his first crop of juveniles, but he is from one of the historic Moyglare Stud's best families, and it would be no surprise if a patient approach paid off with his progeny, just as it did with him.

Night of Thunder (Ire) (Highest Timeform Rating 126)
Dubawi (Ire) – Forest Storm (Galileo (Ire))

Night of Thunder was unbeaten in two starts at two, including a six-furlong listed race at Doncaster, and is perhaps best remembered for causing a surprise in one of the deepest renewals of the 2000 Guineas in recent memory, when beating Kingman and Australia (amongst others) at 40/1. He proved that to be no fluke, though, when placed in the St James's Palace Stakes, Prix du Moulin and Queen Elizabeth II Stakes later that season, and returned at four to record a second Group 1 success in the Lockinge Stakes. Retired to stand at Darley's Kildangan Stud in Ireland for 2016, Night of Thunder's first yearlings—who were bred off a fee of €30,000—averaged £62,352 when going through the ring last year, including the half-brother to Prix de la Foret winner Aclaim, who went the way of Phoenix Thoroughbred for 260,000 guineas, and the three-parts brother to Dubai World Cup winner Prince Bishop, who was bought by Anthony Stroud on behalf of Godolphin for €180,000. Bill Dwan, whose Castlebridge Consignment offered the latter individual, was glowing in his appraisal of the sire ("I've been very impressed with the Night of Thunders, they all seem to have great minds"), and there is seemingly lots to look forward to with the first of his progeny to reach the track this season. Admittedly, the useful-looking Night of Thunder didn't make his debut until the October of his juvenile campaign—he was described by Timeform as still having some filling out to do after winning at Doncaster—but it would still come as a surprise if he didn't supply his fair share of early winners, setting him on a potential path towards leading first-season sire status.

Gleneagles (Ire) (Highest Timeform Rating 125)
Galileo (Ire) – You'resothrilling (USA) (Storm Cat (USA))

Gleneagles won four of his six starts at two, including the National Stakes, and cemented his status as the best three-year-old miler around in 2015 with wins in the English/Irish 2000 Guineas and St James's Palace Stakes. Admittedly, his career on the track finished with something of a whimper—he missed several engagements in the second half of

Gleneagles has all the credentials to make a success of his stallion career

that season on account of the soft ground and finished well held on his final two starts in the Queen Elizabeth II Stakes and Breeders' Cup Classic, respectively—but the form he already had in the book, together with his pedigree (by Galileo and out of a sister to Giant's Causeway, who has produced five stakes winners from her first five foals), guaranteed that he would be well supported when retiring to Coolmore Stud ahead of the 2016 breeding season. Breeders were clearly encouraged by what they saw of his first progeny to go through the ring, too, with his yearlings—who were conceived at a fee of €60,000—selling for an average of £119,495 in 2018, including the record-breaking colt out of the listed winner Lady Eclair. He fetched £380,000 at the Goffs UK Premier Sale, becoming the highest-priced lot in that event's history. It remains to be seen whether there are more records to be broken with Gleneagles when his first runners reach the track this season, but he is very much in the mould of his legendary sire Galileo in appearance, and has all the credentials on paper to enjoy a successful career at stud.

Gutaifan (Ire) (Highest Timeform Rating 117)
Dark Angel (Ire) – Alikhlas (Lahib (USA))

Gutaifan packed a lot into a racing career that lasted only one season, recording the most notable of his four wins (from seven starts) as a juvenile in the Prix Robert-Papin and Flying Childers Stakes. The sort to only do enough when hitting the front—all four of his wins were gained by no further than a head—Gutaifan was retired after finishing down the field in the Prix de l'Abbaye to stand alongside his sire at Yeomanstown Stud, where he covered his first book of mares at a fee of €12,500 in 2016. He went on to prove the best represented first-season sire at the yearling sales, with 107 lots selling at an average of £42,512. The standout result was the half-sister to Group 2 winner Anda Muchacho, who sold to Alistair Donald for €360,000—more than 28 times her sire's stud fee—though she was far from alone, with several other six-figure lots including a half-sister to the Group 1-winning sprinter Battaash (180,000 guineas) and a colt from the family of Queen Mary Stakes winner Signora Cabello (€150,000). A sturdy colt, Gutaifan raced only at five and six furlongs, though both the dam's side of his pedigree (related to the dual Hardwicke Stakes winner Maraahel and Sahool, who was placed in both the Ribblesdale Stakes and Lancashire Oaks) and his relaxed demeanour suggested that he might well have stayed seven given the opportunity. In any case, he looks sure to provide plenty of early winners given his own precocity, and sheer weight of numbers alone—he covered 203 mares in 2016—should guarantee that he features amongst the most successful first-season sires in 2019.

Best of the rest

Another stallion who consistently outperformed his stud fee at the yearling sales was **Hot Streak** (122), with his 51 lots to sell last year doing so at an average of £43,029—more than six times the £7,000 he stood for in his debut season at Tweenhills Stud. He won the Cornwallis Stakes at two and Temple Stakes at three, both over five furlongs, and looks to have just the right sort of profile for first-season sire success. Similar comments apply to **Brazen Beau** (126) and **Outstrip** (116), who covered their first books of mares at Dalham Hall for £10,000 and £5,000, respectively, in 2016. The former was a high-class sprinter in his native Australia who has already achieved notable success with his first runners Down Under, while Outstrip was a precocious talent for Charlie Appleby, winning the Champagne Stakes and Breeders' Cup Juvenile Turf at two, before showing that he had trained on with a good third behind Kingman and Night of Thunder in the following year's St James' Palace Stakes. By Invincible Spirit, who is building an enviable record as a sire of sires, **Cable Bay** (119) was placed in a handful of the most important two-year-old races in 2013, including the Dewhurst, and proved better than ever at the age of four to win the John of Gaunt Stakes and Challenge Stakes. Meanwhile, **Anjaal** (114) and **Ivawood** (118), who won consecutive renewals of the July Stakes for Richard Hannon, are others with outside claims to the title of champion first-season sire, along with the Poule d'Essai des Poulains/Prix de la Foret winner **Make Believe** (127), Diamond Jubilee Stakes runner-up **Due Diligence** (120) and Group 3-winning juvenile **Cappella Sansevero** (109).

SECTION

TIMEFORM'S VIEW

Chosen from the Timeform Formbook, here is Timeform's detailed analysis—compiled by our team of race reporters and supplemented by observations from Timeform's handicappers—of a selection of key juvenile races from last year.

CURRAGH Sunday August 12
GOOD

Keeneland Phoenix Stakes (Group 1)

Pos	Draw	Btn	Horse	Age	Wgt	Eq	Trainer	Jockey	SP
1	1		ADVERTISE	2	9-3		Martyn Meade	Frankie Dettori	11/10f
2	2	½	SO PERFECT (USA)	2	9-0		Aidan O'Brien, Ireland	Seamie Heffernan	7/1
3	3	½	THE IRISH ROVER (IRE)	2	9-3	(t)	Aidan O'Brien, Ireland	Donnacha O'Brien	12/1
4	5	2¾	INDIGO BALANCE (IRE)	2	9-3		Mrs J. Harrington, Ireland	C. T. Keane	14/1
5	4	3	SERGEI PROKOFIEV (CAN)	2	9-3		Aidan O'Brien, Ireland	Ryan Moore	7/4

5 ran Race Time 1m 12.29 Closing Sectional (3.00f): 33.50s (107.9%) Winning Owner: Phoenix Thoroughbred Limited 1

The first Group 1 race for 2-y-os in 2018 was billed as a rematch between the pair that got closest to the now-sidelined Calyx in the Coventry Stakes, but the anticipated duel failed to materialise and this has to go down as a sub-standard renewal, Sergei Prokofiev one of a couple that pulled hard in the early stages, Advertise taking full advantage and ensuring this prestigious prize crossed the Irish Sea for the first time since Princely Heir was successful for Mark Johnston in 1997. **Advertise** didn't need to be at his best to follow up last month's July Stakes victory, taking the step up into Group 1 company in his stride, though helped in no small part by his main market rival underperforming; led first 1f, ridden soon after halfway, led again approaching final 1f, tackled close home, kept going well; should prove at least as effective at 7f, with the National Stakes back here and/or the Dewhurst sure to come under close consideration, especially with Calyx—the only horse to beat Advertise to date—reportedly ruled out for the season. **So Perfect** continues to progress, her Group 3-win here 6 weeks earlier having been given a boost with Skitter Scatter's success in a similar event at Leopardstown since, doing especially well under the circumstances having pulled hard in the early stages; waited with, ridden over 2f out, challenged final 1f, kept on well; should prove as effective at 7f and will get the chance to have another go in a Group 1 contest—this time against her own sex—if taking in Moyglare Stud Stakes on Irish Champions Weekend, with the Group 2 Debutante Stakes here in a fortnight also open to her. **The Irish Rover** who finished some way behind Advertise and Sergei Prokofiev in the Coventry Stakes 8 weeks earlier, seemed to show improved form in first-time tongue strap though was seen to maximum effect; led after 1f and able to dictate at a steady pace, ridden 2f out, headed approaching final 1f, kept on. **Indigo Balance** hasn't gone on since making a winning start in a big-field C&D maiden in May, but he still looked in need of the experience here, unsuited by the way the race developed, and may yet to better; in rear, ridden soon after halfway, hung badly left approaching final 1f, made no impression. **Sergei Prokofiev** was far too free 8 weeks on from chasing home Calyx and Advertise in the Coventry Stakes and is better judged on previous form, though clearly will have a question to answer when next seen, by which time he may not necessarily be at the top of Ballydoyle's 2-y-o pecking order; chased leaders but refused to settle, pushed along over 2f out, hung right approaching final 1f, not persevered with once held.

DEAUVILLE Sunday August 19
GOOD

Darley Prix Morny (Group 1)

Pos	Draw	Btn	Horse	Age	Wgt	Eq	Trainer	Jockey	SP
1	9		PRETTY POLLYANNA	2	8-11		Michael Bell	Silvestre De Sousa	16/10f
2	7	¾	SIGNORA CABELLO (IRE)	2	8-11		John Quinn	Frankie Dettori	43/10
3	6	4	TRUE MASON	2	9-0		K. R. Burke	P. J. McDonald	25/1
4	3	2½	LAND FORCE (IRE)	2	9-0		Aidan O'Brien, Ireland	Ryan Moore	4/1
5	8	hd	SEXY METRO (FR)	2	9-0		D. Guillemin, France	Cristian Demuro	85/10
6	5	3	SIMPLY STRIKING (FR)	2	9-0		M. Delcher Sanchez, France	Stephane Pasquier	88/10
7	2	1½	KINKS	2	9-0		Mick Channon	Charles Bishop	56/1
8	1	1½	COMEDY (IRE)	2	8-11		K. R. Burke	Ben Curtis	88/10
9	4	hd	MARIE'S DIAMOND (IRE)	2	9-0		Mark Johnston	James Doyle	17/1

9 ran   Race Time 1m 10.24   Winning Owner: W. J. and T. C. O. Gredley

Leading colts Calyx and Advertise had been possible runners here at one time, the former missing this and the rest of the year through injury and the latter running in Ireland instead the previous weekend, and it was a pair of fillies who proved much the best, Pretty Pollyanna just the stronger late on to give trainer Michael Bell a second win 24 years after another filly Hoh Magic, the placed pair also representing British trainers who've won this before in a field where the home-trained runners were always up against it numerically. **Pretty Pollyanna** whose form last time is proving strong, confirmed herself the best 2-y-o filly around at present, pushed a lot closer than she had been in the Duchess of Cambridge but up against another smart filly here and the pair of them pulled clear; made running, went with zest, shaken up 2f out, tackled final 1f, found plenty to assert in the closing stages. **Signora Cabello** improved further and emerged from this with plenty of credit, her winning run only ended by another smart and determined filly; tracked pace, ridden under 2f out, challenged final 1f to go upsides halfway inside last, no extra only late on, pulled clear of rest; there are more good races to be won with her. **True Mason** ran to a similar level as last time, confirming himself a useful colt, but finished much further behind Signora Cabello than he had in the Robert Papin; waited with, effort over 1f out, kept on but no match for principals. **Land Force** who's being kept busy, needed to improve further but ran below form, his stable's lack of form well documented but Marie's Diamond, whom he beat in the Richmond, fared even worse here; prominent, ridden over 2f out, not quicken, one paced. **Sexy Metro** dwelt. **Kinks** was well held over 1f longer trip, finding this too competitive; bumped start, held up, beaten over 1f out. **Comedy** had winning run ended but best not judged on this run; alone in racing up stand rail (which was avoided in preceding c/d handicap) which almost certainly wasn't the place to be, showed speed there for a long way but struggling 2f out before dropping away. **Marie's Diamond** who's being kept busy, found run of good form coming to a halt; in touch, ridden over 2f out, soon beaten.

CURRAGH Sunday September 16
GOOD

Moyglare Stud Stakes (Group 1)

Pos	Draw	Btn	Horse	Age	Wgt	Eq	Trainer	Jockey	SP
1	3		SKITTER SCATTER (USA)	2	9-0		P. J. Prendergast, Ireland	R. P. Whelan	7/2f
2	9	2	LADY KAYA (IRE)	2	9-0		Ms Sheila Lavery, Ireland	R. C. Colgan	8/1
3	6	1¼	HERMOSA (IRE)	2	9-0		Aidan O'Brien, Ireland	Seamie Heffernan	20/1
4	10	nk	ZAGITOVA (IRE)	2	9-0		Aidan O'Brien, Ireland	Ryan Moore	4/1
5	1	1½	MAIN EDITION (IRE)	2	9-0		Mark Johnston	Frankie Dettori	5/1
6	7	2¾	BEYOND REASON (IRE)	2	9-0		Charlie Appleby	William Buick	9/2
7	8	2¼	JUST WONDERFUL (USA)	2	9-0		Aidan O'Brien, Ireland	Donnacha O'Brien	9/2
8	2	½	SMART FLIES (IRE)	2	9-0		J. S. Bolger, Ireland	R. P. Cleary	100/1
9	4	1	BANDIUC EILE (IRE)	2	9-0		J. S. Bolger, Ireland	K. J. Manning	40/1
10	5	7	ANGELIC LIGHT (IRE)	2	9-0		M. D. O'Callaghan, Ireland	L. F. Roche	33/1

10 ran Race Time 1m 25.60 Closing Sectional (3.00f): 37.50s (97.8%) Winning Owner: Mr Anthony Rogers & Mrs Sonia Rogers

An average renewal of this Group 1 for fillies that went the way of the one with the best form on offer, Skitter Scatter making it a red-letter day for Patrick Prendergast and Ronan Whelan who were both recording a first ever win at this level; an early pace battle, eventually won by Main Edition, placed the emphasis firmly on stamina. **Skitter Scatter** who has done nothing but improve all year, did so once more to complete a hat-trick of pattern-race wins, again lots to like about this performance, a more patient ride than usual serving to underline her versatility; broke fast, soon settled in mid-division, ridden 2f out, forced to switch 1f out, stayed on to lead final 100 yds, edged left, well on top finish; a credit to connections, her pedigree/style of racing suggests 1m should be within range next year. **Lady Kaya** showed improved form to get closer to the winner than in the Debutante, the way she went through the race suggesting success at this level is no forlorn hope; close up, travelled best, led on bridle over 1f out, collared last ½f, outstayed; pedigree screams speed and is well worth another try at 6f on this evidence. **Hermosa** showed much improved form with a performance that augurs well for the future, very much the type to come into her own at middle distances next year; mid-division, still plenty to do 2f out, ran on late to snatch third in the final strides. **Zagitova** ran to a similar level to last time and would probably have held on for third but for some late interference; prominent, close up second 1f out, looked held when hampered well inside final 1f. **Main Edition** failed by a long chalk to repeat her Sweet Solera form, did too much too soon; made running, headed 2f out, weakened. **Beyond Reason** who arrived here on the back of a pair of pattern-race wins in France, is better judged on that form for now, the writing on the wall a long way out here; chased leaders, driven over 2f out, no extra. **Just Wonderful** a leading contender based on her impressive Group 3 win at this track last time, ran no sort of race, the drop back in trip a mere side issue; waited with, shaken up over 2f out, found little. **Smart Flies** flying too high in this grade, ran as well as entitled to; never involved. **Bandiuc Eile** fared no better than last time under a change of tactics, her Debutante effort very much a standout at this stage; raced well off the pace, beaten long way out. **Angelic Light** who needed to find plenty of improvement, ran poorly; tracked pace, struggling halfway, weakened.

Goffs Vincent O'Brien National Stakes (Group 1)

Pos	Draw	Btn	Horse	Age	Wgt	Eq	Trainer	Jockey	SP
1	7		QUORTO (IRE)	2	9-3		Charlie Appleby	William Buick	11/8f
2	5	1¼	ANTHONY VAN DYCK (IRE)	2	9-3		Aidan O'Brien, Ireland	Ryan Moore	6/4

3	2	4½	CHRISTMAS (IRE)	2	9-3		Aidan O'Brien, Ireland	Emmet McNamara	9/1
4	4	1¾	MOHAWK (IRE)	2	9-3		Aidan O'Brien, Ireland	Seamie Heffernan	16/1
5	3	2¼	LAND FORCE (IRE)	2	9-3		Aidan O'Brien, Ireland	Donnacha O'Brien	8/1
6	6	¾	HIGHLAND FORTUNE (USA)	2	9-3	(b)	J. A. Stack, Ireland	William James Lee	25/1
7	1	ns	WARGRAVE (IRE)	2	9-3		J. A. Stack, Ireland	C. D. Hayes	50/1

7 ran Race Time 1m 24.81 Closing Sectional (3.00f): 35.30s (103.0%) Winning Owner: Godolphin

A strong renewal of this Group 1 featuring a head-to-head between Godolphin's Quorto and Anthony Van Dyck representing team Ballydoyle, the former maintaining his unbeaten record to become the first son of Dubawi—who himself won this very race in 2004—to win a Group 1 as a 2-y-o; Christmas made sure that there was no hanging around but the big 2 had it to themselves from 2f out. **Quorto** continues to look the real deal, following up his Superlative win with another impressive display, one which suggests he'll make into a high-class colt next year; mid-division, loomed up 2f out, went on approaching final 1f, edged right, driven out; the Dewhurst is the obvious next port of call should connections opt to run him again this year. **Anthony Van Dyck** took his form up another notch despite having his winning run ended, kept much closer to the pace than last time but unable to hold off a potential top-notcher; close up, pushed along 3f out, led briefly 2f out, carried right final 1f, no extra late on; will stay at least 1¼m and remains open to improvement with that in mind. **Christmas** ran creditably, clear best of the rest, plenty of merit in that, particularly as he was again asked to do all the donkey work; forced pace, headed 2f out, kept on. **Mohawk** ran respectably, again finishing behind the pair that beat him in the Futurity; mid-division, ridden 2f out, wandered, kept on, never landed a blow. **Land Force** fared no better than last time, beaten before the 1f longer trip became an issue; held up, switched 3f out, effort flattened out. **Highland Fortune** in first-time blinkers, wasn't up to this better company; held up, shaken up 2f out, hung right, weakened. **Wargrave** still a maiden, was flying too high in this grade, needs sights lowering; in rear, left behind 2f out.

NEWMARKET (ROWLEY) Friday September 28
GOOD

Shadwell Rockfel Stakes (Group 2) (1)

Pos	Draw	Btn	Horse	Age	Wgt	Eq	Trainer	Jockey	SP
1	1		JUST WONDERFUL (USA)	2	9-0		Aidan O'Brien, Ireland	Ryan Moore	7/2
2	6	1¾	DANDHU	2	9-0		David Elsworth	Gerald Mosse	12/1
3	5	1½	MAIN EDITION (IRE)	2	9-0		Mark Johnston	Frankie Dettori	15/8f
4	4	2	MODEL GUEST	2	9-0	(s)	George Margarson	Jamie Spencer	25/1
5	2	¾	CANTON QUEEN (IRE)	2	9-0		Richard Hannon	Tom Marquand	10/1
6	3	1½	DUTCH TREAT	2	9-0		Andrew Balding	Oisin Murphy	13/2
7	9	¾	CALIFORNIA LOVE	2	9-0		Richard Spencer	Tom Queally	50/1
8	7	3¼	YOURTIMEISNOW	2	9-0		Roger Varian	Silvestre De Sousa	5/1
9	8	6	AJRAR	2	9-0		Richard Hannon	William Buick	16/1

9 ran Race Time 1m 25.30 Closing Sectional (3.00f): 37.3s (98.0%) Winning Owner: Mr M. Tabor, D. Smith & Mrs John Magnier

The Rockfel tends to be overshadowed in the defining events for 2-y-o fillies, no different this time, a decisive winner but a sub-standard field on the whole, more so with Main Edition again falling below her summer standard, that one setting a sound gallop, the overall leader while a group of 5 raced wider apart. **Just Wonderful** has done it in fits and starts rather than smoothly, but her career curve is clear all the same from her flashpoints, looking the part on her better days, including here, impressive even if the race took less winning than it might, still basically on the bridle when everying else was flat out and shooting ahead approaching the last 1f, not doing much in front, upright at times, hard to crab all the same after what she'd done to the field; she'll be part of the Guineas squad next spring, looking like there's more talent to be unlocked, though she's a Dansili and not a Galileo, but before all that she's a good fit (for the most part) for the Breeders' Cup, given her gears and experience. **Dandhu** in only her second month of racing but rose to the challenge, aimed high straight out of novices, though the performance doesn't quite equate to what a Group 2 runner-up normally looks like, and she was flattered by her proximity to the gearing-down winner, staying on for second in the last 100 yds, albeit emerging from the other group to the pair she split. **Main Edition** same tactics, though more controlled than in the Moyglare, still brushed aside by the winner over 1f out before also run out of second, hard to say she overdid it this time, more likely that she's just lost an edge at this stage of a season which began for her in May and snowballed all the way through to the Sweet Solera; she's not just a 2-y-o on looks. **Model Guest** has done this before (Sweet Solera) in exceeding reasonable expectations in Group company, the run in between when overturned in an Ascot novice as relevant to her status, and she was only sixth 1f out (outpaced in Dip) before closing up again after the boiling point of the race; she was in cheekpieces for the first time. **Canton Queen** ran much the same race as Just Wonderful for a good way, still in third 1f out, only 2l off the lead then, a fairer snapshot than her finishing position, fading as the pressures of the hike in class eventually told, no hiding place in where she raced; she should do well as a 3-y-o. **Dutch Treat** hasn't really looked a Group-class filly in either the May Hill or this, less so here, unimpeded (had been at Doncaster), outpaced when it mattered, time for her sights to be reset. **California Love** hasn't gone on in pattern company since her novice win, scoping dirty after the Sweet Solera but just all at sea in the Dip this time, losing her place quickly. **Yourtimeisnow** fly-jumped leaving the stalls, and the act of revving her up to recover opened a lid that proved her downfall, compounded by going up in trip, refusing to settle, spent by the final 1f. **Ajrar** has been asked a lot since her winning debut, possibly to her detriment, looking low on motivation here, beaten a long way out.

NEWMARKET (ROWLEY) Saturday September 29
GOOD to FIRM

Juddmonte Royal Lodge Stakes (Group 2) (1)

Pos	Draw	Btn	Horse	Age	Wgt	Eq	Trainer	Jockey	SP
1	2		MOHAWK (IRE)	2	9-0		Aidan O'Brien, Ireland	Donnacha O'Brien	8/1
2	3	1¼	SYDNEY OPERA HOUSE	2	9-0		Aidan O'Brien, Ireland	W. M. Lordan	20/1
3	8	1¾	CAPE OF GOOD HOPE (IRE)	2	9-0		Aidan O'Brien, Ireland	Seamie Heffernan	9/2
4	4	1	VICTORY COMMAND (IRE)	2	9-0		Mark Johnston	Silvestre De Sousa	16/1
5	7	2	ARTHUR KITT	2	9-0		Tom Dascombe	Richard Kingscote	11/4
6	10	2¾	DUKE OF HAZZARD (FR)	2	9-0	(t)	Paul Cole	Luke Morris	10/1
7	9	22	BEATBOXER (USA)	2	9-0		John Gosden	Frankie Dettori	7/4f

7 ran   Race Time 1m 36.12   Closing Sectional (3.00f): 35.55s (101.4%)   Winning Owner: Mr D. Smith, Mrs J. Magnier, Mr M. Tabor

That the race was the springboard for Roaring Lion is the exception rather than the rule for the Royal Lodge, tending to fit more in the second division of 2-y-os, this renewal having that feel, a 1-2-3 for Aidan O'Brien but each having already had a go in Group company, and the home challenge wasn't what it looked like being, Arthur Kitt underperforming and something seemingly wrong with favourite Beatboxer; they raced together down the middle of the track, a modest pace quickening sharply after halfway. **Mohawk** expressed himself all the more, mercifully taken out of the firing line of some of the top 2-y-os, behind Anthony Van Dyck the last twice, as well as Quorto in the National, and though there was an element of opportunity-grabbing here the longer trip also made a difference to him, responding whenever asked, striking on over 1f out, comfortable in the end, but only his stable-companions to beat; in the zone, it makes sense to have another go at a Group 1 at this trip this back-end, either at Doncaster or America, acknowledging that he wouldn't square up to a 120-odd juvenile, and likewise, next year, he's set to be more a member of the support team amongst the yard's Derby squad. **Sydney Opera House** came out of the other side of his first Group race (brushed aside by Madhmoon) a better horse, things looking up, as it's all about next year for him, with so much stamina in his pedigree, related to Rekindling amongst other strong stayers; positively ridden, lacked the extra gear of Mohawk out of the Dip but stuck to the task, leaving behind the one with whom he'd disputed the lead (Victory Command); even at this early stage it's easy to see him developing into a St Leger contender. **Cape of Good Hope** possibly had a setback to be absent since chasing home Quorto in the Superlative, the time out perhaps leaving him a little rusty, looking poised 2f out but flat-footed for a while before inching closer late on, still a sense that he's only building up to next year, the fact he's a brother to Highland Reel adding fuel to a fire due to be stoked up more in 2019. **Victory Command** beaten half the distance he was by Too Darn Hot in the Solario, but it's still clear that Group races are beyond his means, taking nothing away from all he did to get here, an achievement these days to win 4 races as a 2-y-o; disputed lead with Sydney Opera House until overwhelmed 1f out, at the longest trip he's faced, though his dam won over 12f. **Arthur Kitt** all positive hitherto, and just ran flat whatever the reason, nothing to do with the trip (should stay, by Camelot), labouring from halfway, finishing a place behind one he was lengths ahead of in the Solario. **Duke of Hazzard** unlucky not to beat Al Hilalee at Deauville, but that was only listed level, not that stepping into pattern company explains away his subdued effort, for all the different pressures, held up last and little impression. **Beatboxer** too bad to be true, something presumably amiss, left behind 3f out, eased off; he'd looked the part in his first 2 starts, and his coming here said plenty, as did the market.

Juddmonte Cheveley Park Stakes (Group 1) (1)

Pos	Draw	Btn	Horse	Age	Wgt	Eq	Trainer	Jockey	SP
1	11		FAIRYLAND (IRE)	2	9-0		Aidan O'Brien, Ireland	Donnacha O'Brien	6/1
2	5	nk	THE MACKEM BULLET (IRE)	2	9-0		Brian Ellison	Oisin Murphy	25/1
3	2	½	SO PERFECT (USA)	2	9-0		Aidan O'Brien, Ireland	Seamie Heffernan	6/1
4	10	1	PRETTY POLLYANNA	2	9-0		Michael Bell	Silvestre De Sousa	6/4f
5	8	½	GOSSAMER WINGS (USA)	2	9-0	(b)	Aidan O'Brien, Ireland	W. M. Lordan	25/1
6	6	nk	LADY KAYA (IRE)	2	9-0		Ms Sheila Lavery, Ireland	Robert Colgan	13/2
7	7	nk	QUEEN OF BERMUDA (IRE)	2	9-0	(t)	William Haggas	James Doyle	16/1
8	9	¾	ANGEL'S HIDEAWAY (IRE)	2	9-0		John Gosden	Robert Havlin	20/1
9	3	hd	COMEDY (IRE)	2	9-0		K. R. Burke	Ben Curtis	40/1
10	1	13	SIGNORA CABELLO (IRE)	2	9-0		John Quinn	Frankie Dettori	7/1
11	4	1¾	NO WAY JOSE (IRE)	2	9-0		Brian Meehan	William Buick	66/1

11 ran   Race Time 1m 10.13 Closing Sectional (3.00f): 34.65s (101.2%) Winning Owner: Mrs E M Stockwell/M Tabor/D Smith

A representative field for this year's Cheveley Park, with most of the winners of the other juvenile fillies pattern sprints taking their chance, and it was the Lowther form that came to the fore, but with less than 3½ lengths separating the first 8, it's hard to see this as a strong renewal, the form no more than on a par for what you would expect for the level, the pair that stood out beforehand on their Morny form against the colts both running below form; the pace was sound, but it still paid to race in the first half of the field. **Fairyland** was strong in the betting and followed up her Lowther success, has progressed well through the ranks, building on that Group 2 win, producing a smart effort to give her trainer a third successive win in the race; in touch, smooth progress over 2f out, led inside final 100 yds, driven out; she's been kept to 6f so far and it's a fair chance she'll prove best at up to this trip—which might make placing her next year difficult—this form a fair way behind the pick of the 2-y-o sprinting colts. **The Mackem Bullet** was back under a fully-fledged rider this time and improved further, again going down only narrowly to Fairyland, but showing that Lowther form was no fluke and that it was perhaps a little better than given credit for at the time; chased leaders, ridden over 2f out, kept going well; she'd been sold privately since last seen, and new connections will surely be delighted with their investment. **So Perfect** has back-to-back placings in a pair of Group 1s on her CV now, progressing again in form terms with this form having more substance to it than the Phoenix, with the stronger pace seeing her to better effect; mid-field, went with zest, ridden over 1f out, every chance inside final 1f, no extra late on; elements of her pedigree suggest she ought to stay further, but she races like a sprinter for the time being. **Pretty Pollyanna** came here as the leading 2-y-o filly, and remains so, the bar she cleared in the Morny unsurpassed by the first 3 here, but a hard race there has perhaps left a mark with Signora Cabello also failing to reproduce it, just all the more laboured this time and never looking like getting to the front (made all for her 2 most recent wins); mid-field, pushed along over 2f out, not quicken; she's been kept to 6f so far, without necessarily looking like an out-and-out sprinter and is certainly worth a crack at a Guineas trial next spring. **Gossamer Wings** back up in trip, produced best effort to date, perhaps finding extra stimulation from the first-time blinkers and arguably deserving of extra credit given this didn't seem to get to the bottom of her; slowly into stride, held up, travelled well, shaken up over 1f out, kept on and never nearer, finishing with running left; she's already had a fair bit of racing, but could be one for her trainer's Breeders' Cup squad, given that experience and her pedigree. **Lady Kaya** back down in trip, failed to build on the promise of her run in the Moyglare, but possibly found this race coming too soon after a hard race there, her finishing effort again lacking somewhat; close up, led briefly over 1f out, effort flattened out; there's plenty of speed in her pedigree and she really ought to prove as effective at 6f as 7f. **Queen of Bermuda** turned out again quickly, ran as well as could be expected, providing further proof that she's a useful filly, and versatile with regards ground too, conditions much quicker than those she won on at Ayr last week; held up, pushed along over 2f out, kept on. **Angel's Hideaway** wasn't disgraced after 5 weeks off, not far below her Princess Margaret form given that she was only just over 3 lengths off the winner for all she never looked like playing a hand in the closing stages; slowly into stride, patiently ridden, effort over 2f out, not quicken; she strikes as one that could be tough to place from hereon, but with black type already gained, it's perhaps a case of job done anyway. **Comedy** got back on track to a certain extent, confirming that she's the useful filly she's looked in France, but basically not up to this level; led until over 1f out, no extra inside final 1f. **Signora Cabello** was easy to back and proved a let-down for the first time in her career, the signs clear from an early stage that she wasn't herself for whatever reason; held up, ridden before halfway, lost place over 1f out; she's had a productive first season, bagging a brace of Group 2s, while her second in the Morny leaves her rated higher than the winner of this, but it could be a case of this much and no more with a view to next year given her pedigree and lack of size. **No Way Jose** was out of her depth, failing to make any impact at all from behind.

LONGCHAMP Sunday October 7
GOOD

Qatar Prix Marcel Boussac - Criterium des Pouliches (Group 1)

Pos	Draw	Btn	Horse	Age	Wgt	Eq	Trainer	Jockey	SP
1	5		LILY'S CANDLE (FR)	2	8-11		Fabrice Vermeulen, France	Pierre-Charles Boudot	27/1
2	3	sn	MATEMATICA (GER)	2	8-11		C. Laffon-Parias, France	Maxime Guyon	11/1
3	2	sn	STAR TERMS	2	8-11		Richard Hannon	Andrea Atzeni	6/1
4	1	½	LAGRANDECATHERINE (FR)	2	8-11		Andrea Marcialis, France	Mickael Barzalona	29/1
5	4	¾	PINK DOGWOOD (IRE)	2	8-11		Aidan O'Brien, Ireland	Ryan Moore	25/10
6	6	½	ROCQUES (FR)	2	8-11		F. Chappet, France	Cristian Demuro	15/10f
7	8	hd	DUBAI BEAUTY (IRE)	2	8-11		Saeed bin Suroor	Oisin Murphy	16/1
8	7	1	CERATONIA	2	8-11		Charlie Appleby	William Buick	45/10

8 ran Race Time 1m 38.98 Winning Owner: Ecurie Normandy Spirit

Connections of all the recent winners were represented again and most of these looked open to improvement, but it was hard to enthuse about the level of form beforehand and the result very much confirmed this as a substandard renewal, an outsider prevailing from a maiden in a blanket finish where a few didn't get the best of runs; even so, the runner-up is a promising filly and it's a bit soon to be writing off some of the others. **Lily's Candle** (Style Vendome half-sister to several winners, including French 1m winner Feel Alive: dam, won over hurdles in France, half-sister to smart winner up to 9f Liliside) cost only €15,000 as a yearling but changed hands for €390,000 at the Arc Sale the previous evening and won her new owner a good chunk of that back in showing further improvement to cause a surprise; patiently ridden, she was still last over 1f out but stayed on well when pulled to the outer to make her run, getting up in the final strides; she hadn't been beaten far against colts in the Rochette here last time, but that wasn't a strong race either and while she's progressed well to date, she'll need to improve further to win any more races at this level next term. **Matematica** (Rock of Gibraltar half-sister to useful French 7f winner Guerriere (by Invincible Spirit) and smart French 2-y-o 1m winner Soustraction out of a French 9f winner) coped well with the step up in grade, building on debut promise, though was understandably still in need of experience after just the one run (beaten a nose in newcomers race over c/d); shuffled back early from a good position which rather lit her up to start with, but travelled well on outer, challenged straight, quickened to lead over 1f out, headed final strides; she's sure to progress further and win races. **Star Terms** ran to a similar level as last time despite not the clearest of runs; tracked pace, kept in behind leader over 2f out and not much room again final 1f but kept on well; she's had the most racing of these but by the right sire (Sea The Stars) to train on well, how far she'll end up staying harder to pin down given her speedy family. **Lagrandecatherine** was long odds once more but, upped again in trip, has improved with each run, particularly as her stamina's been tested more (dam won up to 14.5f); she was another who didn't get the best of runs, held up, not clear run up rail early in straight, but finished well late on after squeezing through. **Pink Dogwood** wasn't disgraced up in grade though enjoyed the run of the race from the front more than some; soon led, quickened 2f out, headed entering final 1f, swamped late on; she's not one to write off by any means, bred to come into her own over middle distances next year, conditions putting the emphasis much more on stamina for her maiden win. **Rocques** was sent off favourite as the unbeaten winner of the main trial but more was required here, even in a substandard renewal, and she lost her unbeaten record; raced mid-division after leading early, effort 2f out, lost place when unable to quicken, finished under hands and heels. **Dubai Beauty** ran better than last time, matching her debut form, but again didn't make much impact in the end; in touch, went with zest, challenged under 2f out, edged right before short of room and no extra inside final 1f. **Ceratonia** without the headgear this time (though wore hood in the preliminaries), came with a similar profile to her half-sister Wild Illusion who won this last year but proved to be a disappointment; pressed leader, went with enthusiasm, every chance early in straight but brushed aside readily from then on, albeit not having much room over 1f out.

Qatar Prix Jean-Luc Lagardere (Grand Criterium) Sponsored By Manateq (Group 1)

Pos	Draw	Btn	Horse	Age	Wgt	Eq	Trainer	Jockey	SP
1	3		ROYAL MARINE (IRE)	2	9-0		Saeed bin Suroor	Oisin Murphy	58/10
2	2	nk	BROOME (IRE)	2	9-0		Aidan O'Brien, Ireland	Ryan Moore	6/1
3	5	¾	ANODOR (FR)	2	9-0		F. Head, France	Aurelien Lemaitre	8/10f
4	1	1¾	BOITRON (FR)	2	9-0		Richard Hannon	Cristian Demuro	35/10
5	6	2	SHAMAN (IRE)	2	9-0		C. Laffon-Parias, France	Maxime Guyon	10/1
6	4	3	DARK JEDI (IRE)	2	9-0		Charles Hills	William Buick	17/1

6 ran   Race Time 1m 39.10   Winning Owner: Godolphin

Not the most competitive renewal of what should be France's top 2-y-o contest, and while representatives of Europe's most powerful 2-y-o strings took the first 2 places, it's unlikely either Royal Marine or Broome are at the top of their respective owners' pecking orders; the winner's a most progressive sort, though, while odds-on favourite Anodor probably needs more use making of him. **Royal Marine** whose form last time is proving strong, overcame the rise in class and is improving in leaps and bounds; chased leader, took his measure over 1f out and was just kept up to his work from then, always on top despite the bare result suggesting there wasn't much in it; he'll go on improving, though this may prove his trip next year too. **Broome** improved further, the forcing tactics this time suiting this long-striding galloper, but he again came up against a rapid improver; forced pace, tried to press on before home turn, headed over 1f out, stuck to task when headed though probably flattered a bit by the margin he was beaten; he'll be suited by 1¼m, the Criterium de Saint-Cloud making plenty of appeal. **Anodor** improved a little more despite losing his unbeaten record at odds on, arguably not seen to best effect; in touch, travelled strongly, still third when not quicken over 1f out but was closing on first 2 at the line, possibly unsuited by the change of tactics having made all last time; he's not one to write off, and will stay further than 1m. **Boitron** upped in trip, ran no more than respectably in losing his unbeaten record, disappointing given the step up in trip could have been expected to suit; held up, kept on in straight but no impression on the 3 who raced ahead of him; should prove suited by at least 1m. **Shaman** had shaped well when third to Anodor last time but just ran to a similar level here; held up, not settle fully, ran on, never a threat. **Dark Jedi** played little part up in grade; in rear, always behind.

NEWMARKET (ROWLEY) Friday October 12
GOOD to FIRM

bet365 Fillies' Mile (Group 1) (1)

Pos	Draw	Btn	Horse	Age	Wgt	Eq	Trainer	Jockey	SP
1	7		IRIDESSA (IRE)	2	9-0		Joseph Patrick O'Brien, Ireland	W. M. Lordan	14/1
2	3	1½	HERMOSA (IRE)	2	9-0		Aidan O'Brien, Ireland	Donnacha O'Brien	5/2f
3	4	¾	PRETTY POLLYANNA	2	9-0		Michael Bell	Daniel Tudhope	7/2
4	6	4	SHAMBOLIC (IRE)	2	9-0		John Gosden	Frankie Dettori	14/1
5	2	8	ZAGITOVA (IRE)	2	9-0		Aidan O'Brien, Ireland	Seamie Heffernan	5/1
6	8	2	LAYALEENA (IRE)	2	9-0		Sir Michael Stoute	Jim Crowley	20/1
7	5	sh	BEYOND REASON (IRE)	2	9-0		Charlie Appleby	William Buick	9/1
8	1	6	ANTONIA DE VEGA (IRE)	2	9-0		Ralph Beckett	Harry Bentley	5/1

8 ran   Race Time 1m 38.80   Closing Sectional (3.00f): 37.00s (100.1%)   Winning Owner: Mrs C. C. Regalado-Gonzalez

The most valuable race for 2-y-o fillies in the British programme, one that has gone from strength to strength since the inauguration of the Future Champions meeting, the multiple Group 1 winners Minding and Laurens having won the race in the last 3 years, split by a renewal in which the first 3 have all won at the highest level subsequently, this running certainly up to standard and with the first 3 all having something to recommend them for next year; the race tested stamina to the full and the winner clearly relished that, her success a significant boost for her Derby-winning sire from his relatively small first crop. **Iridessa** up in grade, showed much improved form on her fourth start to spring a surprise, well suited by the emphasis on stamina back at 1m, her performance suggesting she's more likely to make into a Oaks contender than Guineas one; patiently ridden, travelled well, headway when short of room 2f out, stayed on to lead 1f out, in command last ½f, ridden out; a smart filly, with plenty about her physically, and open to further improvement. **Hermosa** strong in the betting, over 1f longer trip, ran her best race, beaten by a stout stayer who came from off the pace, much more likely than that filly to make an impact in the Guineas, though sure to stay further than 1m as well; never far away, every chance and stuck to her task well from 2f out, not quicken last ½f; a smart filly, sure to be worthy of consideration in classic trials in the spring. **Pretty Pollyanna** upped markedly in trip, failed to match the form she showed in mid-summer, though given this came less than 2 weeks after the Cheveley Park, she acquitted herself pretty well, doing plenty and just beaten by 2 stronger stayers; close up, travelled well, led over 2f out, headed 1f out, no extra final 100 yds; this trip looked too far at this stage of her career, but there's little to lose by giving her a Guineas prep next spring and she shouldn't be dismissed out of hand for that assignment. **Shambolic** faced a stiffer task in this grade and ran about as well as she had previously, though she turned in a pretty lacklustre display; held up, labouring 3f out, headway over 1f out, not quicken inside final 1f, never on terms; she may yet do better at 3 yrs, particularly over further. **Zagitova** was below form, seemingly not herself, too keen early and ill at ease on the track after halfway; waited with, not settle fully, ridden 3f out, left behind 2f out; she's best judged on previous form, her physique suggesting she'll really come into her own at 3 yrs. **Layaleena** failed to take the eye beforehand (starey in coat) and was simply flying too high in this grade, particularly on the back of a disappointing second run; waited with, ridden over 3f out, left behind soon after. **Beyond Reason** more exposed than the rest, was well held over 1f longer trip, surely doing too much too soon having also proved edgy and sweated up beforehand; soon led, headed over 2f out, weakened soon after; she should stay at least 1m. **Antonia de Vega** had won a race that hasn't worked out particularly at Goodwood and didn't have quite the chance the market suggested, but she just ran no sort of race after 7 weeks off, in trouble from the off, failing to handle the track at all and reportedly finishing lame; slowly into stride, raced off the pace, never travelling well, left behind over 2f out; she should stay 1m; best judged on previous form.

NEWMARKET (ROWLEY) Saturday October 13
GOOD to FIRM

Masar Godolphin Autumn Stakes (Group 3) (1)

Pos	Draw	Btn	Horse	Age	Wgt	Eq	Trainer	Jockey	SP
1	9		PERSIAN KING (IRE)	2	9-1		A. Fabre, France	Pierre-Charles Boudot	6/5f
2	7	nk	MAGNA GRECIA (IRE)	2	9-1		Aidan O'Brien, Ireland	Donnacha O'Brien	3/1
3	5	3	CIRCUS MAXIMUS (IRE)	2	9-1		Aidan O'Brien, Ireland	Seamie Heffernan	8/1
4	3	3¼	WESTERN AUSTRALIA (IRE)	2	9-1	(t)	Aidan O'Brien, Ireland	W. M. Lordan	12/1
5	4	1	BOERHAN	2	9-1		William Haggas	Jim Crowley	14/1
6	1	10	OMNIVEGA (FR)	2	9-1		David Simcock	Stevie Donohoe	33/1
7	8	12	MASSAM	2	9-1		Mark Johnston	Silvestre De Sousa	8/1
8	2	17	FELIX THE POET	2	9-1		Archie Watson	Hollie Doyle	20/1

8 ran Race Time 1m 37.35 Closing Sectional (3.00f): 36.40s (100.3%) Winning Owner: Ballymore Thoroughbred Ltd

The recent history of the Autumn Stakes is rich, Kingston Hill probably the most celebrated winner after his subsequent St Leger success, whilst Best Solution who won this in 2015 has also gone on to land a Group 1 and last year's winner, Ghaiyyath, remains an exciting prospect; the market was dominated by 2 colts that had made very favourable impressions en route and it was that pair that both upped their game to fight out a thilling finish to an above-average renewal, Persian King and Magna Grecia credited with smart efforts that are above the standard threshold for the race; the pace was sound and there were no hard-luck stories. **Persian King** had created a very good impression with 2 wide-margin wins in France and confirmed himself a most progressive colt with a smart performance to make a successful step up into Group company, made to work harder in the end than looked likely for much of the race, the undulations of the track perhaps playing a part in that, but in a battle for the first time he showed resolution and may have had more to spare than the margin of a neck suggests; tracked pace, travelled strongly, switched over 2f out, led entering final 1f, edged left to the rail, briefly looked vulnerable but proved determined; physically he's the sort to strengthen into a big frame into his 3-y-o season and is potentially a high-class colt. **Magna Grecia** put up a big performance less than 2 weeks on from his impressive winning debut, coping with the step up in grade to make a more experienced and already high-achieving colt work hard, showing much improved form; mid-division, shaken up over 3f out, headway soon after, challenged over 1f out, kept on well and pulled clear of the remainder; he's a powerful individual physically and seems sure to better this smart rating in his 3-y-o season. **Circus Maximus** is a very well-bred colt who's going the right way, no match only for a pair of smart rivals, and he'll learn more from this, especially as he was racing on firmish ground for the first time; chased leaders, led under pressure 2f out, headed entering final 1f, one paced. **Western Australia** wasn't disgraced but is starting to look exposed, no excuses here or last time; chased leader, pushed along over 3f out, led briefly over 2f out, dropped away. **Boerhan** faced a stiff task in this grade, his rating not yet high enough to warrant a crack at Group company; held up, effort 3f out, beaten over 1f out, effort flattened out. **Omnivega** caught the eye on debut but not to the extent that he'd earnt this rise in class, flying too high; in rear, struggling over 2f out, made no impression; he'll still improve a lot but needs to be in calmer waters for now. **Massam** was found out in better company having won a couple of uncompetitive nurseries; led until over 2f out, weakened. **Felix The Poet** clearly wasn't 100% on the day; raced off the pace, weakened over 2f out, eased off.

Darley Dewhurst Stakes (Group 1) (1)

Pos	Draw	Btn	Horse	Age	Wgt	Eq	Trainer	Jockey	SP
1	5		TOO DARN HOT	2	9-1		John Gosden	Frankie Dettori	1/1f
2	1	2¾	ADVERTISE	2	9-1		Martyn Meade	Oisin Murphy	7/1
3	2	1¼	ANTHONY VAN DYCK (IRE)	2	9-1		Aidan O'Brien, Ireland	Donnacha O'Brien	11/4
4	7	4½	SANGARIUS	2	9-1		Sir Michael Stoute	William Buick	8/1
5	6	sh	KUWAIT CURRENCY (USA)	2	9-1		Richard Hannon	Tom Marquand	50/1
6	3	3	CHRISTMAS (IRE)	2	9-1		Aidan O'Brien, Ireland	Seamie Heffernan	20/1
7	4	sh	MOHAWK (IRE)	2	9-1		Aidan O'Brien, Ireland	W. M. Lordan	20/1

7 ran Race Time 1m 24.35 Closing Sectional (3.00f): 35.45s (102.0%) Winning Owner: Lord Lloyd Webber

The pre-eminent race for juveniles in Britain and even without the notable absentees, Quorto and Ten Sovereigns, this was a strong Dewhurst, featuring in Too Darn Hot and Anthony Van Dyck 2 colts that had already reached the 120s on ratings, joined by the hitherto unbeaten Sangarius, a Group 1 winner already in Advertise and recent Royal Lodge winner Mohawk; with a trio of Galileos from Ballydoyle in the field it's not surprising that operation were keen to avoid a muddling race and Christmas pressed on, setting a sound pace that made for a fair test, the result on the day very solid as there was nothing in the way of trouble in-running to report either. **Too Darn Hot** from day one has looked Champion 2-y-o material, mindful from the outset of his outstanding credentials on pedigree, and he completed the perfect season with the best Dewhurst performance since the legendary Frankel in 2010, beating a strong field with authority despite things not going as smoothly as they might have through the race, taking a keen hold early as Dettori sought cover, and then when switched out entering the Dip he briefly looked in trouble, feeling the whip and edging left, perhaps just a sign of immaturity, also getting accustomed to the undulations, on ground that was firmer than he'd encountered before, but after that brief moment of vulnerability—underlined by an in-running price on Betfair that hit a high of 8.0—he flew through the final 1f to take up the running and forge clear impressively; his rating sits in advance of the standard required to win a typical 2000 Guineas, so even in a stellar crop, he sets the bar very high, and there's an expectation that his form will continue to accelerate, especially back at 1m next spring, no quibbling with his position as clear favourite for 2019's first classic, but there'd be more doubt as to whether beyond that he'll develop into a Derby horse, admittedly from a family of middle-distance performers but clearly a fast colt, not the biggest either, and he's already breaking the family mould by showing such speed and precocity; whatever his optimum trip proves to be, though, he has vast talent and is a fantastically exciting prospect. **Advertise** had been rather overlooked in the build up despite already having a Group 1 in the bag, testament to the strength of the race, but close to the off there was money for him and he improved his form further 8 weeks on from the Phoenix, unfortunate to be around in such a stellar year as his rating is as good as some Dewhurst winners; prominent, travelled fluently, challenged 2f out, led briefly entering final 1f, kept on but no match for winner; his pedigree says more sprinter than miler but he saw this extra furlong out well enough at this early stage of his career to at least think it feasible he may prove effective over 1m as a 3-y-o. **Anthony Van Dyck** didn't look quite so well as at the Curragh, getting increasingly warm and wasn't quite able to match his National Stakes rating despite finishing placed in another Group 1 and, typical of a Galileo, his future looks sure to be back over at least 1m and probably further next year; chased leader, led over 2f out, headed entering final 1f, one paced, needs the emphasis more on stamina; he has been kept busy and it's not out of the question that he'll get his chance back up in trip in the Futurity at Doncaster in a couple of weeks. **Sangarius** was taking a big step up into a hot Dewhurst and found it all a bit too much too soon, his relative inexperience showing in the final third of the race, but the involvement at this level should only bring him on; in touch, travelled well, switched over 2f out, not quicken over 1f out, left behind, not unduly punished; physically he'll develop a lot into his 3-y-o season, with a big frame to fill, and he remains a colt with lots of potential. **Kuwait Currency** has been progressing but faced a stiff task in this grade and ran about as well as entitled to, matching his listed-winning form but not having the class to land a serious blow; held up, pushed along 3f out, outpaced 2f out, kept on; he appreciated stepping up to 1m last time and will benefit from a return to that trip. **Christmas** is better than this, nothing wrong with his form in Ireland, and perhaps the ground was firmer than ideal, although his main role seemed to be as pacemaker anyway; made running, headed over 2f out, weakened. **Mohawk** was below form 2 weeks on from winning the Royal Lodge over 1m here, outpaced around 2f out and dropping away; he's not the most physically imposing.

DONCASTER Saturday October 27
GOOD

Vertem Futurity Trophy Stakes (Group 1) (1)

Pos	Draw	Btn	Horse	Age	Wgt	Eq	Trainer	Jockey	SP
1	11		MAGNA GRECIA (IRE)	2	9-1		Aidan O'Brien, Ireland	Donnacha O'Brien	2/1f
2	4	hd	PHOENIX OF SPAIN (IRE)	2	9-1		Charles Hills	Jamie Spencer	11/2
3	8	¾	WESTERN AUSTRALIA (IRE)	2	9-1	(t)	Aidan O'Brien, Ireland	Michael C. Hussey	50/1
4	9	sh	CIRCUS MAXIMUS (IRE)	2	9-1		Aidan O'Brien, Ireland	W. M. Lordan	16/1
5	3	nk	GREAT SCOT	2	9-1		Tom Dascombe	Richard Kingscote	14/1
6	5	2	KICK ON	2	9-1		John Gosden	Kieran O'Neill	16/1
7	1	1½	TURGENEV	2	9-1		John Gosden	Frankie Dettori	7/2
8	6	1¾	DASHING WILLOUGHBY	2	9-1		Andrew Balding	David Probert	16/1
9	10	1½	KING OTTOKAR (FR)	2	9-1		Charlie Fellowes	Ben Curtis	20/1
10	2	2½	RAAKIB ALHAWA (IRE)	2	9-1		David Simcock	Andrea Atzeni	6/1
11	7	11	KUWAIT CURRENCY (USA)	2	9-1		Richard Hannon	Tom Marquand	33/1

11 ran Race Time 1m 37.72 Closing Sectional (3.00f): 37.35s (98.1%) Winning Owner: Smith/Magnier/Tabor/Flaxman Stables

The juvenile Group 1s in Britain and Ireland this autumn have been of a high standard, much less so this one, low even by race standards, capped by the fact there was little over a length separating the first 5 at the line, but the winner is definitely on the classic path for next year, and one or two others in the field will spring up all the more then, too; a fair pace quickened appreciably over 1f out, Western Australia and Circus Maximus teaming up for that move, briefly opening up a gap before those from the pack that were able enough got involved for the final 1f, the pace-pushing pair edging left—influenced in part by the strong crosswind—and shoving Magna Grecia across with a knock-on effect to Phoenix of Spain, resulting in a stewards enquiry, no doubt all the same who the best horse was. **Magna Grecia** did it only narrowly and in a substandard renewal, but this is an instance where the end-of-year rating doesn't adequately tell his story, squeezing into a month what few 2-y-os manage in an entire season, only fortnights spacing his 3 races, going into the Autumn Stakes as a virtual novice and coming out of the scrap against Persian King with an extra edge that got him home on top here, under pressure to chase down the leaders over 2f out and responding all the time, pushed left while joining them (and in turn nudging Phoenix of Spain) but finding extra when it mattered, fostering the feeling that it wasn't quite the scramble for him that a finish of heads and necks makes out; regards the classics, this performance won't do much to reduce any temptation to try Ten Sovereigns in a Guineas, though Anthony Van Dyck is yet to complete his business for the year; he's one of very few at Ballydoyle by Invincible Spirit, whose best progeny have been sprinters or milers, Kingman amongst them, and Magna Grecia doesn't look in the mould of a Derby horse, albeit out of a Galileo mare (Cabaret) who got to 105 as a 2-y-o but failed to train on (still contested the Oaks). **Phoenix of Spain** excellent first season, though the promotional material reads rather better than the rating, getting closer to Too Darn Hot than any 2-y-o has and failing by only a head to win this Group 1, the Champagne hardly a real reflection of the relationship that day and landing on a fairly weak renewal here, giving Magna Grecia all he could handle (but only ¾l ahead of a 50/1 outsider at the line), getting a brief bump off him (effectively caused by others) while chellenging inside the final 1f, having come from further back, seeing out the trip strongly, opening a door to 1¼m next year, lining up for the big leagues, though the classics may be beyond his means. **Western Australia** big difference in him from the Autumn Stakes, measurable in real terms against Magna Grecia and Circus Maximus, much closer to the former and reversing placings with the latter, setting the pace but not a pacemaker as such, in it to win it himself, the fact he went just a fair gallop for the first half accentuating the advantage that a rush got him over 3f out, trying hard to the end, making the absolute most of his control of the race, dangerous to assume it flatters him given who he's with and how he's bred; in common with most of the Australias seen so far, it looks like he'll stay further next year. **Circus Maximus** by Galileo (unlike his stablemates ahead of him) and out of a mare who took off as a 3-y-o, making more progress (over further) in 2019 almost a certainty, in line with the way his first season has gone, reducing two-thirds of the deficit on Magna Grecia from the Autumn Stakes, Western Australia's jump getting him between them this time, to do with dictating, but Circus Maximus was second-best positioned, the first to chase him; all being well, he's bound to be reappearing in an early Derby trial. **Great Scot** made it this far without racing all that efficiently, 3 wins along the way, those habits persisting, clearly possessing a big engine to finish as close as he did, from so far back, anchored in rear but still keen to begin with, a sweep down the far flank (one step ahead of Phoenix of Spain) getting him virtually upsides ½f out. **Kick On** light on experience, coming straight out of maidens, hardly seeing a rival for his Newmarket win but held up this time, all part of the eductaion, and his naivety was exposed by the injection of pace over 3f out, unable to counter it, but pushing through it will do him plenty of good, his final 1f very encouraging, still closing come the line, a tough lesson learned rather than a sign of would-be stamina, not bred to get much further. **Turgenev** ran much the same race as Magna Grecia for 7f, making ground at the same time/rate, that one crossing him 1f out, Turgenev coming to the end of his tether then anyway, not at all the disappointment it might seem from his SP, as this was a big leap from novice company, as impressive as he'd been; he's got all the priviliges to regain the progressive thread as a 3-y-o, by Dubawi out of th 119-rated Tasaday, who was Group 1-placed at 1¼m/1½m for Godolphin, including on fast ground, something Turgenev is yet to face. **Dashing Willoughby** simply found this too much at his stage, much like the winner from the conditions race at Newbury, never better than mid-field, outpaced over 1f out; it's possible this involvement will put him on the front foot for next year, when he should stay very well, by Nathaniel out of a 1½m winner. **King Ottokar** excusably overawed in a race like this for only his second start, no impact, though that he was set the task says something; Shoot For Gold was one of a few subsequent winners in his wake at Newbury, promise likely to be realised next year. **Raakib Alhawa** strength in the market spoke volumes, but the climb was simply too steep, coming here straight from his debut win (when Dashing Willoughby was second), the task increased by being switched and dropped in behind from the start, never getting into the race, but it should still serve a purpose of sorts, having it all ahead of him next year. **Kuwait Currency** had contested the Dewhurst, seemingly taking it out of him, as this was too bad to br true despite another stiff task, chasing the leader until losing his place quickly 3f out.

CHURCHILL DOWNS Friday November 2
GOOD to SOFT

Breeders' Cup Juvenile Fillies Turf (Grade 1)

Pos	Draw	Btn	Horse	Age	Wgt	Eq	Trainer	Jockey	SP
1	6		NEWSPAPEROFRECORD (IRE)	2	8-10		Chad C. Brown, USA	Irad Ortiz, Jr	6/10f
2	14	6¾	EAST	2	8-10		Kevin Ryan	Jamie Spencer	122/10
3	7	nk	STELLAR AGENT (USA)	2	8-10		Jorge R. Abreu, USA	Manuel Franco	716/10
4	4	¾	JUST WONDERFUL (USA)	2	8-10		Aidan O'Brien, Ireland	Ryan Moore	134/10
5	9	½	VARENKA (USA)	2	8-10		H. Graham Motion, USA	Jose L. Ortiz	403/10
6	2	hd	THE MACKEM BULLET (IRE)	2	8-10		Brian Ellison	Oisin Murphy	251/10
7	8	1	BELLE LAURA (USA)	2	8-10		Norm Casse, USA	Julien R. Leparoux	508/10
8	1	1¾	CONCRETE ROSE (USA)	2	8-10		George R. Arnold II, USA	Jose Lezcano	77/10
9	13	ns	MY GAL BETTY (USA)	2	8-10		Roger L. Attfield, Canada	Javier Castellano	202/10
10	5	4¼	LA PELOSA (IRE)	2	8-10		Charlie Appleby	William Buick	184/10
11	10	hd	PAKHET (USA)	2	8-10		Todd A. Pletcher, USA	John R. Velazquez	409/10
12	3	1½	LILY'S CANDLE (FR)	2	8-10		Fabrice Vermeulen, France	Pierre-Charles Boudot	115/10
13	12	hd	SUMMERING (USA)	2	8-10		Thomas F. Proctor, USA	Drayden Van Dyke	285/10
14	11	3¾	LADY PRANCEALOT (IRE)	2	8-10		Richard Baltas, USA	Joseph Talamo	627/10

14 ran   Race Time 1m 39.00   Closing Sectional (2f): 25.25s (98.0%)   Winning Owner: Klaravich Stables

In the 6 previous runnings of this as a Grade 1 the average rating of the winner has been 112, and that's including Lady Eli's spike in 2014 when she won by 2¾l, necessary context for assessing Newspaperofrecord, who broke through the 120-barrier with her breathtaking performance, dominant from start to finish. **Newspaperofrecord** (200,000Y: by Lope de Vega: third foal: half-sister to smart 6f winner Classical Times (by Lawman): dam, winner up to 7f (2-y-o 6f winner), closely related to smart 5f/6f winner Udontdodou) is a turf filly the like of which American racing has rarely ever seen at her stage, no other way to put it after a phenomenal performance where she ran riot in the face of her biggest test yet, let loose on the lead and soon opening up once asked in the straight, and the margin could have been 10l had she been ridden right out rather than geared down in the last ½f; there's no 2-y-o filly in Europe that can touch her, and Royal Ascot may well be on her agenda next summer according to her trainer, who sourced her at the Tattersalls Sales last October; Newspaperofrecord looks something special indeed, crowning a breakthrough season for her sire Lope de Vega. **East** had made her debut only a little over 5 weeks previously, some going to get to this point so soon, not only experience against her but also the draw, widest of all, dropped out last before cutting through the field in the straight, getting second in the last strides, first home in the democratic race, Newspaperofrecord in a league of her own. **Stellar Agent** has been a distant third behind Newspaperofrecord the last twice, though this represents personal progress by her, hopelessly chasing the winner over 1f out, losing second in the final stride. **Just Wonderful** failed to fully replicate her Rockfel form but didn't do at all badly from the position she was in (after a slowish start), making up more ground than all bar East in the straight, Newspaperofrecord skewing things slightly, everything else made to look more ordinary than they probably are. **Varenka** came here as a maiden, though splitting Newspaperofrecord and Stellar Agent the time before, no chance of getting to even the latter this time from where she raced (in the rear division), staying on late. **The Mackem Bullet** has been one of the stories of the season for her rise from humble beginnings to her seconds in the Lowther and Cheveley Park, below that level here but seemingly seeing out the trip from mid-field. **La Pelosa** hasn't come forward at all since the Albany, the Natalma at Woodbine a Grade 1 in name only, ridden differently here, weakening after giving chase to Newspaperofrecord. **Lily's Candle** came over the top in a scramble for a substandard Marcel Boussac, nowhere near a Group 1-standard of rating out of it, her limitations exposed more here, never involved.

Breeders' Cup Juvenile Turf (Grade 1)

Pos	Draw	Btn	Horse	Age	Wgt	Eq	Trainer	Jockey	SP
1	5		LINE OF DUTY (IRE)	2	8-10		Charlie Appleby	William Buick	35/10
2	2	½	UNCLE BENNY (USA)	2	8-10		Jason C. Servis, USA	Irad Ortiz, Jr	80/10
3	7	nk	SOMELIKEITHOTBROWN (USA)	2	8-10	(b)	Michael J. Maker, USA	Jose L. Ortiz	150/10
4	1	1¾	ARTHUR KITT	2	8-10		Tom Dascombe	Richard Kingscote	342/10
5	10	1	WAR OF WILL (USA)	2	8-10		Mark E. Casse, North America	Joel Rosario	157/10
6	4	¾	FORTY UNDER (USA)	2	8-10		Jeremiah C. Englehart, USA	Manuel Franco	64/10
7	12	2	CURRENT (USA)	2	8-10		Todd A. Pletcher, USA	John R. Velazquez	94/10
8	9	hd	THE BLACK ALBUM (FR)	2	8-10		Mme J.Soubagne, France	Mickael Barzalona	302/10
9	14	hd	ANTHONY VAN DYCK (IRE)	2	8-10		Aidan O'Brien, Ireland	Ryan Moore	31/10f
10	8	2	OPRY (USA)	2	8-10		Todd A. Pletcher, USA	Javier Castellano	286/10
11	13	4½	MARIE'S DIAMOND (IRE)	2	8-10		Mark Johnston	Florent Geroux	475/10

12	11	hd	KING OF SPEED (USA)	2	8-10	(b)	Jeff Bonde, USA	Gary L. Stevens	211/10
13	6	4½	HENLEY'S JOY (USA)	2	8-10	(b)	Michael J. Maker, USA	Tyler Gaffalione	119/10
14	3	hd	MUCH BETTER (USA)	2	8-10		Bob Baffert, USA	Drayden Van Dyke	170/10

14 ran Race Time 1m 40.06 Closing Sectional (2f): 26.46s (94.5%) Winning Owner: Godolphin

An eighth European winner in 12 runnings of the Juvenile Turf and a second for Charlie Appleby, though Line of Duty looks a significantly brighter prospect than his 2013 winner Outstrip; a sound gallop coupled with fairly testing conditions ensured a test of stamina by American turf standards and there were some tired horses in the closing stages, the first 2 both wandering late on and the winner having to survive an enquiry. **Line of Duty** had his win at Chantilly last month boosted 6 days earlier when Wonderment (third that day) won the Criterium de Saint-Cloud and did his own bit for the form by landing this big prize, proving well suited by a relative test of stamina; mid-field, ridden over 2f out, headway over 1f out, hung left and bumped rival final 1f, led final 50 yds, stayed on well; by Galileo, he'll be suited by middle distances in 2019 and will be well worth his place in a Derby trial in the spring, his form after this at about the same standard as his Derby-winning stable-companion Masar (an unlucky sixth in this in 2018) had achieved this time last year, if a bit short of what the best 2-y-os have done back home in Europe. **Uncle Benny** unbeaten in his first 2 starts (on dirt then turf, over 5f and 6f respectively) showed much improved form, suited by a stiffer test of stamina over this longer trip, no great surprise given his pedigree; dwelt, mid-field, not clear run over 2f out, headway under pressure over 1f out, wandered, every chance when bumped final 100 yds, ran on. **Somelikeithotbrown** showed improved form, reversing placings from last time with the sixth, going down fighting from the front; made running, effort under 2f out, caught final 50 yds. **Arthur Kitt** ran creditably, proving his effectiveness over 1m at the second attempt; in touch, ridden over 2f out, kept on but never looked like winning. **Anthony Van Dyck** was below form, more than anything leaving the impression he's had enough for the year, a wide draw no help either, clearly better judged on what he's done in Europe when next we see him; held up, off the bridle long way out, driven over 2f out, made no impression; he'll be suited by this far and further in 2019. **Marie's Diamond** was always out the back, not good enough but perhaps also a race too far in a season that began in April; he's bred to stay this far.

TIMEFORM'S BEST OF 2018

Juveniles

Too Darn Hot (127p). The name of Britain's leading two-year-old could hardly have been more appropriate after a sweltering summer, one in which John Gosden's charge swept all before him, winning all four of his starts and looking a likely candidate to head the ratings long before he concluded his campaign with a clear-cut defeat of Phoenix winner **Advertise** (119) and National Stakes runner-up **Anthony Van Dyck** (118) in the Dewhurst. The top four two-year-old colts all went into winter quarters unbeaten, the others being **Quorto** (122p), who took his winning sequence to three in the aforementioned National Stakes, Too Darn Hot's stablemate **Calyx** (120p), an exciting winner of the Coventry who was sidelined by injury but is expected to make a full recovery, and the Middle Park winner **Ten Sovereigns** (120p), the pick of the Ballydoyle juveniles.

The best two-year-old in France was the Andre Fabre-trained **Persian King** (117p), though his best performance came on British soil, when beating subsequent Vertem Futurity Trophy winner **Magna Grecia** (116p) in the Autumn Stakes at Newmarket. By way of reply, British-trained horses won 13 of the French two-year-old pattern races, with the Godolphin trio of **Line of Duty** (112p), **Royal Marine** (113p) and **Royal Meeting** (114p) perhaps chief amongst them. The former won the Prix de Conde at Chantilly in October for Charlie Appleby, before going on to add the Breeders' Cup Juvenile Turf to his tally the following month, while Royal Marine and Royal Meeting provided their trainer Saeed bin Suroor with two of his nine Group 1 wins in the latest season, in the Prix Jean-Luc Lagardere and Criterium International, respectively.

The two-year-old fillies were a less impressive group, headed by the one-two from the Prix Morny, **Pretty Pollyanna** (116) and **Signora Cabello** (113), the Fillies' Mile heroine **Iridessa** (113p), and **Skitter Scatter** (113p), who capped a fine year with a ready success in the Moyglare Stud Stakes. **Fairyland** (112) was Ballydoyle's highest-rated juvenile filly courtesy of her Cheveley Park success, while there was a surprise win in the Prix Marcel Boussac for the rags-to-riches French filly **Lily's Candle** (104), who cost only €15,000 as a yearling, but made significantly more when changing hands for €390,000 the night before her Longchamp success. She failed to reproduce that form when subsequently well held in the Breeder's Cup Juvenile Fillies Turf, though it is unlikely to have made any difference to the result, with **Newspaperofrecord** (122p) running out a hugely impressive winner for US trainer Chad Brown; the prospect of her coming to Royal Ascot for the Coronation Stakes is one to savour.

Sprinters

Honours were shared in the sprinting division, with the ten Group 1 sprints for three-year-olds and upwards in Europe all going the way of different horses. They did not include the pick of the previous year's excellent crop, **Battaash** (133) and **Harry Angel** (131), though that pair still proved themselves to be the best around, when giving weight and a beating to their rivals in Group 2 events. The former is set to return in 2019, but Harry Angel was retired after his second behind **Sands of Mali** (125) in the Champions Sprint Stakes. That represented a career-best effort for the Richard-Fahey trained Sands of Mali, who had previously finished a close-up second behind **Eqtidaar** (117) in the Commonwealth Cup at Royal Ascot, while the other major sprints at that meeting, the King's Stand Stakes and the Diamond Jubilee Stakes, went the way of Godolphin's **Blue Point** (129) and the Ballydoyle import from Australia **Merchant Navy** (126), respectively.

The July Cup also had Aidan O'Brien's name on it courtesy of the three-year-old **U S Navy Flag** (125), while the Flying Five Stakes—the first renewal of the race since its elevation to Group 1 status—was won by another member of the classic generation in the shape of **Havana Grey** (118), confirming the promise of his fourth in the Nunthorpe. He was beaten two and three quarter lengths at York, but there was no such daylight between **Alpha Delphini** (121) and **Mabs Cross** (118) as they flashed past the post

Alpha Delphini edges the verdict from Mabs Cross (noseband) in last year's Nunthorpe

together in one of the races of the season, with the judge taking several minutes to conclude that the former had got the verdict by a pixel. It was a difficult result to take for connections of Mabs Cross, but she belatedly gained the victory her consistency all season deserved, when signing off with a narrow victory in the Prix de l'Abbaye.

A special mention must also go to **The Tin Min** (125), who won a Group 1 for the third year in succession, the Sprint Cup joining trophies for the 2016 Champions Sprint and 2017 Diamond Jubilee on his mantelpiece. French trainer Freddie Head can boast a similarly decorated CV—both as a jockey and in his second career—and he won the other Group 1 sprint in Europe, the Prix Maurice de Gheest, for a magnificent seventh time in the latest season, with **Polydream** (122) staying on strongly to add to Marchand d'Or and Moonlight Cloud's three wins apiece.

Milers

The specialist milers in 2018 were much of a muchness, with the obvious exception of **Alpha Centauri** (128). She provided trainer Jessica Harrington with a first classic victory in the Irish 1000 Guineas, and went on to establish herself as the best at this distance in Europe when beating the colts, including the subsequent Prix du Moulin winner **Recoletos** (125), in the Prix Jacques le Marois. Sadly, Alpha Centauri suffered an injury when bidding for her fifth consecutive Group 1 win in the Matron Stakes, notably faltering when coming to challenge eventual winner **Laurens** (120) a furlong out, and was subsequently retired. Laurens had already won the Prix Saint-Alary and Prix de Diane, both over a mile and a quarter, in the first half of the campaign, but she proved better than ever when dropping back to a mile in the autumn, going on to match Alpha Centauri's four Group 1 wins with a typically game success in the Sun Chariot Stakes at Newmarket in October.

Saxon Warrior (124) provided Aidan O'Brien with a ninth success in the 2000 Guineas, but failed to add to his tally in five subsequent starts over longer trips. In hindsight, it may have been that a mile was his optimum trip, but sadly we never got the chance to find out; he was also retired after suffering a tendon injury on Irish Champions Weekend. In a rather damning indictment of last season's three-year-old milers, several of the other Guineas winners in Europe also failed to win again, notably the 66/1 winner of the 1000 Guineas, **Billesdon Brook** (114), and **Romanised** (121), who was a breakthrough winner of the Irish 2000 Guineas for Ken Condon's small stable, but had his limitations exposed subsequently, including when only sixth behind **Without Parole** (122) in the St James's Palace Stakes at Royal Ascot. Ultimately, it was **Expert Eye** (124) who laid down the best end-of-season marker amongst his crop, when signing off with a last-gasp triumph in the Breeders' Cup Mile.

Seven-year-old **Lightning Spear** (124) finally gained an elusive Group 1 win in the Sussex Stakes, that coming after good placed efforts in the Lockinge (when beaten just a nose by **Rhododendron** (120)) and the Queen Anne (when third behind **Accidental Agent** (122) and **Lord Glitters** (121)). Meanwhile, the brilliant **Winx** (134) won over distances ranging from seven to ten furlongs in 2018, including a record fourth win in the Cox Plate, Australia's premier weight-for-age race (by two lengths from multiple Group 1 winner **Benbatl** (129)). She is included in this section, however, having produced her best effort over the mile of the Chipping Norton Stakes at Randwick, when winning by seven lengths with the minimum of fuss.

Middle-distances

The sweltering conditions and prolonged drought was bad news for connections of **Cracksman** (136), whose best form is with cut in the ground, meaning that he saw less action than expected in 2018. Nevertheless, he still ended the season as Timeform's highest-rated horse in training, earning his figure—for the second year in succession—with a runaway win in the Champion Stakes at Ascot (by six lengths from Hardwicke winner **Crystal Ocean** (129)). British Champions' Day proved a red-letter occasion for the Clarehaven yard of John Gosden, with **Roaring Lion** (130) making light of the drop back to a mile to win the Queen Elizabeth II Stakes. Timeform's Horse of the Year, Roaring Lion ended the season with four Group 1 wins to his name after being beaten

Roaring Lion was crowned Timeform's Horse of the Year in 2018

in both the 2000 Guineas and the Derby, with his best performance coming when readily beating Prince of Wales's Stakes/King George winner **Poet's Word** (129) by three and a quarter lengths in the Juddmonte International.

British Champions' Day also saw **Magical** (128) announce herself as a major force with a clear-cut victory in the Fillies' & Mares' Stakes, and she took another significant step forward when chasing home Clarehaven's outstanding filly **Enable** (134) in the following month's Breeders' Cup Turf. Enable bypassed Ascot to wait for the Breeders' Cup after winning Europe's most valuable race, the Prix de l'Arc de Triomphe, for the second year running, scrambling home from the unlucky Irish Oaks winner **Sea of Class** (129) after an interrupted preparation. Enable became the first Arc winner to go on to win at the Breeders' Cup meeting in the same year, and she stays in training—along with Sea of Class—to try to win a third Arc in 2019, a feat never previously accomplished.

Only Godolphin's trainers could rival John Gosden's dominance of the latest season, with a four-timer on Dubai World Cup night—including Saeed bin Suroor's eighth Dubai World Cup win with **Thunder Snow** (126), who went on to finish third behind **Accelerate** (131) in the Breeders' Cup Classic—proving a portent of things to come. On the domestic front, Charlie Appleby saddled the long-awaited first Derby winner to carry the Godolphin royal blue, with 2000 Guineas third **Masar** (125) running out a smooth winner from another Darley homebred, the Mark Johnston-trained **Dee Ex Bee** (121). Sadly, Masar missed the second half of 2018 through injury, but **Wild Illusion** (120)—who ran a big race herself at Epsom, when finishing second to **Forever Together** (117) in the Oaks—picked up the slack in admirable fashion for Appleby, recording back-to-back Group 1 wins in the Nassau Stakes and Prix de l'Opera. Dee Ex Bee, on the other hand, failed to reproduce his Epsom form when lining up in the Irish Derby at the Curragh, leaving **Latrobe** (119) to spring a historic 14/1-surprise for Joseph and Donnacha O'Brien, while **Study of Man** (122) came out on top in a bunched finish to the French equivalent, the Prix du Jockey Club.

Looking further afield, **Justify** (129) became the 13th winner of America's Triple Crown, while **Almond Eye** (126) completed the fillies' equivalent in her native Japan. The former, who was unraced at two, was retired after his Belmont Stakes victory due to an ankle injury, but there is seemingly still plenty to look forward to with Almond Eye. She ended last season with a first defeat of her elders in the Japan Cup, and seemingly has the Arc—and a mouth-watering clash with Enable—on her agenda in 2019.

Stayers

John Gosden also won the Long Distance Cup on British Champions' Day courtesy of **Stradivarius** (127), who was securing his fifth win from as many starts last season and arguably the least important of them all; indeed, the hard work had already been done by the time he arrived at Ascot, with his first four wins—in the Yorkshire Cup, Ascot

Stradivarius (right) comes out on top in a thrilling renewal of the Ascot Gold Cup

Gold Cup, Goodwood Cup and Lonsdale Cup—being the ones that saw him land the inaugural WH Stayers' Million. His arrival on the staying scene could hardly have been better timed to support the BHA's welcome move to improve opportunities for the long-distances horses, and he'll be hard to topple again in 2019.

The Gold Cup was undoubtedly the most thrilling of Stradivarius' wins, with first **Torcedor** (123) and then the more patiently-ridden French raider **Vazirabad** (123) forcing him to pull out all the stops. **Order of St George** (128)—the winner in 2016 and runner-up in 2017—could manage only fourth in the latest renewal and, having been retired to stud subsequently, it remains to be seen who will be Ballydoyle's chief representative in the staying ranks in 2019. They certainly aren't short on options, with **Kew Gardens** (127) having shown stamina to be his forte when winning a strong renewal of the St Leger (by two and a quarter lengths from the promising filly **Lah Ti Dar** (122)), just 24 hours before **Flag of Honour** (123) made all the running to land the Irish equivalent at the Curragh.

Finally, Prix du Cadran winner **Call The Wind** (122) and **Holdthasigreen** (124), who capped a fine season in the big staying races in France by winning the Prix Royal-Oak, are others to watch in 2019, but perhaps the most interesting of the pretenders to Stradivarius' throne is **Cross Counter** (124). Trained by that man Charlie Appleby, Cross Counter led home a historic, British-trained one-two-three in the Melbourne Cup and, still relatively unexposed at staying trips, he could be a big player in this division in years to come.

WANT TO KNOW THE SCORE?

info**gol**

The football analyst at your fingertips

See the beautiful game differently with the Infogol analytics App. Bet smarter with expected goal stats onside.

Scores ✛ Stats ✛ Tips ✛ Features

Visit infogol.net & download the free App today

2018 STATISTICS

TRAINERS (1,2,3 earnings)		Horses	Indiv'l Wnrs	Races Won	Runs	% Strike Rate	Stakes £
1	John Gosden	219	119	178	705	25.2	8,288,597
2	Aidan O'Brien, Ireland	96	21	24	229	10.5	5,461,634
3	Sir Michael Stoute	120	54	77	426	18.1	4,433,616
4	Mark Johnston	227	115	226	1,440	15.7	3,970,316
5	Charlie Appleby	121	61	88	313	28.1	3,552,308
6	Richard Fahey	256	132	190	1,599	11.9	3,097,749
7	William Haggas	175	96	145	657	22.1	2,905,361
8	Richard Hannon	289	117	172	1,401	12.3	2,855,956
9	Andrew Balding	183	82	123	772	15.9	2,329,863
10	Roger Varian	175	75	106	603	17.6	1,894,302

JOCKEYS (by winners)		1st	2nd	3rd	Unpl	Total Rides	% Strike Rate
1	Oisin Murphy	198	179	155	598	1130	17.5
2	Silvestre De Sousa	176	133	109	517	935	18.8
3	James Doyle	156	99	72	306	633	24.6
4	Luke Morris	150	169	155	1046	1520	9.9
5	Joe Fanning	137	140	105	553	935	14.7
6	Jim Crowley	130	93	77	403	703	18.5
7	Robert Havlin	127	97	99	356	678	18.7
8	Adam Kirby	123	111	98	462	794	15.5
9	P. J. McDonald	120	112	101	558	891	13.5
10	Daniel Tudhope	116	101	86	394	697	16.6

SIRES OF WINNERS (1,2,3 earnings)		Races Won	Runs	% Strike Rate	Stakes £
1	Dubawi (by Dubai Millennium)	128	625	20.5	3,573,742
2	Galileo (by Sadler's Wells)	43	456	9.4	3,058,599
3	Frankel (by Galileo)	70	305	23.0	2,977,256
4	Sea The Stars (by Cape Cross)	67	341	19.6	2,794,678
5	Kodiac (by Danehill)	180	1565	11.5	2,486,230
6	Poet's Voice (by Dubawi)	97	744	13.0	2,358,344
7	Kitten's Joy (by El Prado)	20	121	16.5	2,221,258
8	Dark Angel (by Acclamation)	144	1236	11.7	2,216,748
9	Invincible Spirit (by Green Desert)	110	822	13.4	1,857,549
10	Acclamation (by Royal Applause)	106	967	11.0	1,801,502

LEADING HORSES (1,2,3 earnings)		Races Won	Runs	Stakes £
1	Roaring Lion 3 gr.c Kitten's Joy – Vionnet	4	7	1,968,044
2	Poet's Word 5 b.h Poet's Voice – Whirly Bird	3	4	1,403,280
3	Cracksman 4 b.c Frankel – Rhadegunda	2	3	1,136,662
4	Stradivarius 4 ch.c Sea The Stars – Private Life	5	5	1,088,833
5	Masar 3 ch.c New Approach – Khawlah	2	3	938,476
6	Crystal Ocean 4 b.c Sea The Stars – Crystal Star	3	6	791,693
7	Lightning Spear 7 ch.h Pivotal – Atlantic Destiny	1	4	738,313
8	Kew Gardens 3 b.c Galileo – Chelsea Rose	2	6	570,271
9	Sands of Mali 3 b.c Panis – Kadiania	2	5	517,230
10	Wild Illusion 3 b.f Dubawi – Rumh	1	4	490,760

SECTION

THE TIMEFORM TOP 100

2 Year Olds

127p	Too Darn Hot
122p	Newspaperofrecord (f)
122p	Quorto
120p	Calyx
120p	Ten Sovereigns
119	Advertise
118	Anthony Van Dyck
118	Jash
117p	Persian King
116p	Magna Grecia
116	Pretty Pollyanna (f)
115p	Madhmoon
115p	San Donato
115	Soldier's Call
114p	Royal Meeting
114	Phoenix of Spain
114	Sergei Prokofiev
113p	Iridessa (f)
113p	Japan
113p	Royal Marine
113p	Skitter Scatter (f)
113	Kessaar
113	Signora Cabello (f)
112p	Circus Maximus
112p	Hello Youmzain
112p	Line of Duty
112	Boitron
112	Broome
112	Fairyland (f)
112	Western Australia
111p	Mount Everest
111	Barbill
111	Christmas
111	Graignes
111	Great Scot
111	Sydney Opera House
111	The Mackem Bullet (f)
110p	Khaadem
110p	Mohaather
110p	Red Impression (f)
110	Anodor
110	Guaranteed
110	Rumble Inthejungle
109p	Wonderment (f)
109	Emaraaty Ana
109	Fox Tal
109	Hermosa (f)
109	Just Wonderful (f)
109	Land Force
109	Mohawk
109	So Perfect (f)
109	Well Done Fox
108p	Masaff
108p	Shang Shang Shang (f)
108	Arctic Sound
108	Dark Vision
108	Sexy Metro
108	Vange
107p	Fleeting (f)
107p	Natalie's Joy (f)
107p	Norway
107p	Sangarius
107	Lady Kaya (f)
107	Legends of War
107	No Needs Never
107	Pocket Dynamo
106p	Donjah (f)
106p	East (f)
106p	Kick On
106p	Turgenev
106	Arthur Kitt
106	Swissterious
106	Vintage Brut
105p	Mission Boy
105	Duke of Hazzard
105	Main Edition (f)
105	Marie's Diamond
105	Quiet Endeavour
105	Shine So Bright
105	True Mason
105	Watan
104p	Dubai Warrior
104p	Noble Moon
104p	Shades of Blue (f)
104	Azano
104	Bye Bye Hong Kong
104	Cardini
104	Chuck Willis
104	Gossamer Wings (f)
104	Konchek
104	Kuwait Currency
104	Lily's Candle (f)
104	Sovereign
104?	The Irish Rover
103p	Cape of Good Hope
103p	Nivaldo
103	Angel's Hideaway (f)
103	Charming Kid
103	Dunkerron
103	La Pelosa (f)
103	Star Terms (f)
103	Van Beethoven
103	Zagitova (f)

3 Year Olds

130	Roaring Lion
129	Justify
129	Sea of Class (f)
128	Alpha Centauri (f)
128	Magical (f)
127	Kew Gardens
126	Almond Eye (f)
125p	Young Rascal
125	Masar
125	Sands of Mali
125	U S Navy Flag
125	Wissahickon
124	Cross Counter
124	Expert Eye
124	Saxon Warrior
123	Brundtland
123	Flag of Honour
123	Gustav Klimt
123	James Garfield
123	Mendelssohn
122	Gronkowski
122	I Can Fly (f)
122	Lah Ti Dar (f)
122	Nelson
122	Old Persian
122	Ostilio
122	Polydream (f)
122	Study of Man
122	Wind Chimes (f)
122	Without Parole
121	Dee Ex Bee
121	Hunting Horn
121	Knight To Behold
121	Romanised
120	Corinthia Knight
120	Happily (f)
120	Laurens (f)
120	Loxley
120	Tantheem (f)
120	Vintager
120	Wild Illusion (f)
119p	Astronomer
119p	Ghaiyyath
119p	Sir Erec
119	Intellogent
119	Latrobe
119	With You (f)
118p	Wadilsafa
118	Ancient Spirit
118	Cascadian
118	Communique
118	Havana Grey
118	Hey Jonesy
118	Lost Treasure
118	Rostropovich
118	Tip Two Win
117p	Urban Beat
117	Eqtidaar
117	Forever Together (f)
117	Glorious Journey
117	Homerique (f)
117	Invincible Army
117	Kenya
117	Magic Wand (f)
117	Mer Et Nuages
117	Olmedo
117	Patascoy
117	Raymond Tusk
117	Royal Youmzain
117	Sioux Nation
117	Southern France
116	Cardsharp

116	Elarqam	132	Beauty Generation	123	Marmelo	120	Cliffs of Moher
116	Emaraaty	132	Gun Runner	123	Mirage Dancer	120	Count Octave
116	First Contact	131	Accelerate	123	Salouen	120	Desert Encounter
116	Fleet Review	131	Harry Angel	123	Torcedor	120	Finche
116	Giuseppe Garibaldi	129	Benbatl	123	Vazirabad	120	Folkswood
116	Hey Gaman	129	Blue Point	123	Yucatan	120	Gifted Master
116	Sheikha Reika (f)	129	Crystal Ocean	122	Accidental Agent	120	Ice Breeze
116	Snazzy Jazzy	129	Enable (f)	122	Bound For Nowhere	120	Khan
116	Wootton	129	Ertijaal	122	Call The Wind	120	Rhododendron (f)
116	Yafta	129	Poet's Word	122	Dschingis Secret	120	Sharja Bridge
115p	Tabdeed	129	West Coast	122	Heavy Metal	120	Sir Dancealot
115	Equilateral	128	Cloth of Stars	122	Inns of Court	120	Way To Paris
115	Hazapour	127	Redkirk Warrior	122	Limato	120	Weekender
115	Laugh A Minute	127	Stradivarius	122	Magic Circle	119	Above The Rest
115	Nyaleti (f)	127	Waldgeist	122	Monarchs Glen	119	Almodovar
115	Proschema	126	Merchant Navy	122	Mustashry	119	Anda Muchacho
115	Speak In Colours	126	Redzel	122	Subway Dancer	119	Barsanti
115	The King	126	Thunder Snow	122	Thundering Blue	119	Comicas
114	Altyn Orda (f)	126	Yoshida	122	Wuheida (f)	119	Coronet (f)
114	Ben Vrackie	125	Best Solution	121	Addeybb	119	Finsbury Square
114	Billesdon Brook (f)	125	Mind Your Biscuits	121	Alpha Delphini	119	Forest Ranger
114	Encrypted	125	Recoletos	121	Beat The Bank	119	Gold Vibe
114	Gold Town	125	The Tin Man	121	Called To The Bar	119	Laraaib
114	Key Victory	124	Blair House	121	Century Dream	119	Leshlaa
114	Mootasadir	124	Capri	121	Desert Skyline	119	Mustajeer
114	Regal Reality	124	City Light	121	Dutch Connection	119	One Master (f)
114	Wells Farhh Go	124	Defoe	121	Jordan Sport	119	Sheikhzayedroad
114	Weltstar	124	Holdthasigreen	121	Lord Glitters	119	Sound Check
114	Zaaki	124	Iquitos	121	Muntahaa	119	Spirit of Valor
114	Zaman	124	Lightning Spear	121	Order of St George	119	Stormy Antarctic
		124	North America	121	Plumatic	119	Tarboosh
		123	Brando	121	Rare Rhythm	119	Tiberian
		123	Hawkbill	121	Royal Line	119	Washington DC

Older Horses

136	Cracksman
134	Winx (f)
133	Battaash

123	Jungle Cat
123	Kachy
123	Lancaster Bomber

121	Talismanic
121§	Frontiersman
120	Caspian Prince

* Indicates best performance achieved in a race other than a hunter chase

PROMISING HORSES

A p symbol is used by Timeform to denote horses we believe are capable of improvement, with a P symbol suggesting a horse is capable of much better form. Below is a list of selected British- and Irish-trained horses with a p or P, listed under their current trainers.

CHARLIE APPLEBY

Al Hilalee 2 b.c.	102p
Art Song (USA) 2 b.c.	88p
Court Poet 2 b.c.	99p
Divine Image (USA) 2 ch.f.	88p
Enchanting Man 2 ch.g.	79p
Jalmoud 2 ch.c.	85p
Line of Duty (IRE) 2 ch.c.	112p
Lover's Knot 2 b.f.	90p
Marhaban (IRE) 2 b.c.	70p
Moonlight Spirit (IRE) 2 b.c.	88p
Nashirah 2 b.f.	84p
Orchid Star 2 b.f.	84p
Quorto (IRE) 2 b.c.	122p
Space Blues (IRE) 2 ch.c.	102p
Star Safari 2 b.c.	88p
Summer Flair (IRE) 2 gr.f.	75P
Velorum (IRE) 2 b.c.	90p
Wings of Time 2 b.g.	52p
Zakouski 2 b.c.	100p
Aurum (IRE) 3 b.c.	96p
Auxerre (IRE) 3 b.c.	110p
Ghaiyyath (IRE) 3 b.c.	119p
Ispolini 3 b.g.	107p
Sayf Shamal (USA) 3 ch.f.	81p

ANDREW BALDING

Bangkok (IRE) 2 b.c.	91p
Barossa Red (IRE) 2 ch.g.	82p
Bell Rock 2 b.c.	89p
Be More 2 b.f.	73p
Boutonniere (USA) 2 b.g.	68p
Dashing Willoughby 2 b.c.	102p
Dudley's Boy 2 b.c.	77p
Edinburgh Castle (IRE) 2 b.c.	75p
Flashcard (IRE) 2 b.g.	97p
Fox Leicester (IRE) 2 gr.c.	87p
Fox Shinji 2 b.c.	65p
Good Birthday (IRE) 2 b.c.	83p
Grace And Danger (IRE) 2 b.f.	91p
Happy Power (IRE) 2 gr.c.	99p
Hero Hero (IRE) 2 b.c.	89p
King Power 2 ch.f.	66p
Landa Beach (IRE) 2 b.c.	87p
Luck of Clover 2 b.f.	55p
Never Do Nothing (IRE) 2 b.c.	83p
Paradise Boy (IRE) 2 ch.c.	74p
Purdey's Gift 2 b.c.	73p
Raise You (IRE) 2 ch.c.	93p
Rectory Road 2 b.g.	87p
Rux Power 2 b.f.	81p
Sawasdee (IRE) 2 br.c.	69p
Sea Sculpture 2 b.c.	70p
Top Power (FR) 2 ch.c.	70p

Berkshire Blue (IRE) 3 b.g.	107p
Iconic Girl 3 b.f.	63p
Private Cashier 3 b.f.	76p
Sovrano 3 ch.g.	69p
Urban Aspect 3 b.g.	110p
Young Bernie 3 b.g.	51p

RALPH BECKETT

Brasca 2 ch.g.	73p
Cabarita 2 ch.f.	64p
Chaleur 2 b.f.	102p
Chartered 2 b.f.	80p
Copal 2 b.g.	80p
Dancing Vega (IRE) 2 ch.f.	99P
Fancy Dress (IRE) 2 gr.f.	51p
Fearless Warrior (FR) 2 ch.c.	88p
Feliciana de Vega 2 b.f.	100p
Fragrant Belle 2 ch.f.	79p
Glance 2 b.f.	91p
Gold Arrow 2 b.f.	86p
Innocent (IRE) 2 b.f.	78p
Isabella Brant (FR) 2 gr.f.	76p
Loch Lady 2 b.f.	57p
Manuela de Vega (IRE) 2 b.f.	98p
Nivaldo (IRE) 2 b.c.	103p
Oydis 2 b.f.	67p
Philonikia 2 b.f.	65p
Princess Salamah (IRE) 2 ch.f.	72p
Queen Power (IRE) 2 ch.f.	89p
Rowland Ward 2 b.c.	75p
Sam Cooke (IRE) 2 b.g.	86p
Skymax (GER) 2 b.g.	89p
Stormwave (IRE) 2 b.c.	82p
Cecchini (IRE) 3 b.f.	101p
Rock Eagle 3 ch.g.	107p

MICHAEL BELL

Allmankind 2 b.c.	91p
Babbo's Boy (IRE) 2 gr. or ro.c.	75p
Brelades Bay (IRE) 2 br.f.	60p
Dubai Philosopher (FR) 2 b.c.	76p
Eagles By Day (IRE) 2 b. or br.c.	81p
Eightsome Reel 2 b.f.	84p
Emirates Empire (IRE) 2 b.c.	70p
L'Un Deux Trois (IRE) 2 gr.c.	73p
Lucky Turn (IRE) 2 b.f.	68p
Master Brewer (FR) 2 b.g.	95p
Nuremberg (IRE) 2 b.g.	84p
Youthful 2 b.g.	77p
Plait 3 ch.f.	83p

MARCO BOTTI

Capla Flyer 2 b.f.	58p
Fox Coach (IRE) 2 br.g.	96p
Geizy Teizy (IRE) 2 b.f.	73p

Guroor 2 ch.f.	78p
Mandy The One 2 b.f.	72p
Oliveto (FR) 2 b.c.	82p
Roma Bangkok 2 b.c.	94p
Sonja Henie (IRE) 2 b.f.	79p
Tofan 3 ch.c.	80p
Yusra 3 b.f.	87p

K. R. BURKE

Beautiful Gesture 2 ch.f.	68p
Chasing The Rain 2 b.f.	77p
Dawn Blaze 2 ch.g.	58p
High Contrast 2 b.g.	59p
Kadar (USA) 2 b. or br.c.	95p
Self Assessment (IRE) 2 b.f.	85p
Lord Oberon 3 b.g.	109p

OWEN BURROWS

Almokhtaar (USA) 2 b.g.	61p
Baasem (USA) 2 ch.g.	75p
Badayel (IRE) 2 ch.c.	86p
Dawaam (USA) 2 b.f.	94p
Eithaar 2 b.f.	74p
Furqaan (IRE) 2 b.f.	73p
Muraad (IRE) 2 gr.g.	81p
Raheeb (IRE) 2 b.f.	82p
Watheerah (USA) 2 b.f.	88p
Alfarqad (USA) 3 b. or br.g.	80p
Anasheed 3 b.f.	98p
Elwazir 3 ch.c.	109p
Habub (USA) 3 b.c.	94p
Kasbaan 3 br.g.	97p
Motaraabet 3 b.g.	83p
Mutaaqeb 3 b.c.	103p
Sawwaah 3 b.c.	102p
Tabdeed 3 ch.c.	115p
Wadilsafa 3 b.c.	118p

HENRY CANDY

Alfred Boucher 2 gr.g.	87p
Maiden Castle 2 b.f.	67p
Quarry Beach 2 b.f.	73p
Cleverley (IRE) 3 gr.f.	59p
Great Midge 3 b.g.	82p
Ornamental 3 ch.c.	85p
Skill Set (IRE) 3 b.f.	88p
Let Rip (IRE) 4 b.g.	84p

MICK CHANNON

Chairmanoftheboard (IRE) 2 b.c.	96p
Dear Miriam (IRE) 2 b.f.	58p
Modern Millie 2 b.f.	69P
Swinging Jean 2 b.f.	74p
The Night Porter 3 b.g.	99p

ROGER CHARLTON

Catan (GER) 2 b.g.	98p
Creationist (USA) 2 b.c.	75p
Fashion's Star (IRE) 2 ch.f.	88P
Great Bear 2 b.c.	81p
Headman 2 b.c.	96p
Il Capitano (FR) 2 ch.c.	75p
Infuse (IRE) 2 b.f.	68p
Junior Rip (IRE) 2 b.g.	59p
Lady Adelaide (IRE) 2 b.f.	83p
Mojave 2 b.g.	60p
Mubariz 2 b.c.	95p
Qarasu (IRE) 2 br.c.	83p
Red Impression 2 gr.f.	110p
Royal Star 2 b.f.	74p
Skyman 2 b.c.	81p
Tempus 2 b.c.	88P
Thorn 2 b.c.	84p
Total Commitment (IRE) 2 b.c.	80p
Yimkin (IRE) 2 b.f.	69p
Herculean 3 ch.c.	102p
Perpetrator (IRE) 3 b.g.	82p

PAUL COLE

Aristomachos (IRE) 2 b.c.	77p
High Commissioner (IRE) 2 ch.c.	76P
Mercenary Rose (IRE) 2 b.f.	75p
Parish Poet (IRE) 2 ch.f.	78p
Shir Khan 2 ch.c.	89p

ROBERT COWELL

Bhangra 2 br.f.	54p
Rocket Action 2 b.c.	96p

CLIVE COX

Aigiarne (IRE) 2 b.f.	59p
Dargel (IRE) 2 b.c.	67p
Designated 2 ch.f.	66p
Glorious Emaraty (FR) 2 b.g.	81p
House of Kings (IRE) 2 b.c.	89p
Just The Man (FR) 2 b.c.	76p
Lethal Lover 2 b.f.	62p
Meghan Sparkle (IRE) 2 b.f.	63P
Pour Me A Drink 2 ch.c.	76p
Red Armada (IRE) 2 b.c.	86p
Regal Ambition (IRE) 2 b.f.	65p
Remembering You (IRE) 2 b.f.	61p
Shades of Blue (IRE) 2 br.f.	104p
Vasiliev 2 ch.c.	86p
Venture (IRE) 2 b.c.	67p
Wise Counsel 2 b.c.	94p
Ask The Dude (IRE) 3 ch.g.	69p
Hulcote 3 b.f.	90p

Icart Point 3 br.g. ... 95p
Isle of Man 3 b.c. ... 63p
Tamerlane (IRE) 3 b.g. ... 84p

SIMON CRISFORD
Alnadir (USA) 2 ch.c. ... 85p
Approach The City (IRE) 2 b.c. ... 73p
Asad (IRE) 2 ch.c. ... 79p
Buniann (IRE) 2 b.c. ... 71p
Dreaming Away (IRE) 2 b.f. ... 74p
Ebbraam 2 b.f. ... 82p
Eden Gardens (IRE) 2 ch.g. ... 86p
Imperial Charm 2 b.f. ... 91p
Kareena Kapoor (USA) 2 ch.f. ... 79p
Say The Word 2 b.g. ... 73p
Starry Eyes (USA) 2 ch.f. ... 81p
Turn 'N Twirl (USA) 2 b.f. ... 81p
Turntable 2 b.g. ... 68p
Wallaa 2 b.f. ... 74p
Wise Ruler 2 ch.c. ... 81p
Cuban Fire (IRE) 3 ch.f. ... 57p
Iron Dove (IRE) 3 gr.f. ... 50p
Mutafani 3 b.c. ... 103p
Outbox 3 b.g. ... 110p
Persian Sun 3 b.g. ... 84p
Reconcile (IRE) 3 b.g. ... 83p
Romaana 3 b.f. ... 89p
Sajanjl 3 ch.f. ... 74p
Shikoba (IRE) 3 b.f. ... 58p
Well Suited (IRE) 3 ch.c. ... 94p

KEITH DALGLEISH
Boston George (IRE) 2 b.c. ... 80p
Dark Lochnagar (USA) 2 b.c. ... 82p
Gometra Ginty (IRE) 2 b.f. ... 56p
I Could Do Better (IRE) 2 b.g. ... 85p
Iron Mike 2 gr.c. ... 73p
Summer Daydream (IRE) 2 b.f. ... 93p

TOM DASCOMBE
Artistic Streak 2 b.f. ... 60p
Flighty Almighty 2 b.f. ... 64p

MICHAEL DODS
Beaufort (IRE) 2 b.g. ... 72p
Dutch Pursuit (IRE) 2 b.g. ... 77p
Myrmidons (IRE) 2 ch.g. ... 77p
Pendleton 2 b.c. ... 78p

ED DUNLOP
Achaeus (GER) 2 b.c. ... 60p
Global Destination (IRE) 2 b.c. ... 66p
Global Express 2 ch.c. ... 73p
Global Warning 2 b.c. ... 76p
Jabalaly (IRE) 2 b.c. ... 80p
Melodies 3 ch.f. ... 94p

TIM EASTERBY
Arletta Star 2 b.f. ... 64p
Cheeky Lola (IRE) 2 b.f. ... 55p
Gremoboy 2 ch.c. ... 75p
Ugo Gregory 2 br.g. ... 60p

DAVID ELSWORTH
Arabian King 2 ch.c. ... 73p
No Nonsense 2 b.c. ... 82p
Target Zone 2 ch.c. ... 66p

RICHARD FAHEY
Allen A Dale (IRE) 2 br.c. ... 71p
Arctic Fox 2 ch.f. ... 68p
Coolagh Forest (IRE) 2 b.c. ... 75p
Doris Bleasedale (IRE) 2 b.f. ... 57p
Eljayeff (IRE) 2 b.c. ... 90p
Irreverent 2 b.c. ... 81p
Jungle Secret (IRE) 2 ch.f. ... 59p
Menin Gate (IRE) 2 gr.g. ... 61p
More Than This 2 b.c. ... 100p
Ramesses 2 b.g. ... 71p
Red Hot (FR) 2 b.f. ... 72p
War Tiger (USA) 2 b.c. ... 73p
Borodin (IRE) 3 b.g. ... 98p
Claire Underwood (IRE) 3 b.f. ... 89p

JAMES FANSHAWE
Audarya (FR) 2 b.f. ... 89p
Carnival Rose 2 b.f. ... 72p
Durrell 2 b.g. ... 81p
Edifice 2 b.f. ... 70p
Entrusting 2 b.c. ... 73p
Keyhaven 2 b.c. ... 73p
Knowing 2 b.c. ... 71p
Pamper 2 b.f. ... 54p
Chetwynd Abbey 3 b.f. ... 64p
Harry's Bar 3 ch.c. ... 69p
Indian Tygress 3 b.f. ... 96p
Spanish Archer (FR) 3 b.g. ... 103p
The Pinto Kid (FR) 3 b.g. ... 90p
Tiger Eye (IRE) 3 b.f. ... 73p
Flaming Marvel (IRE) 4 b.g. ... 91p

CHARLIE FELLOWES
Faro Angel (IRE) 2 b.g. ... 93p
I Am Magical 2 b.f. ... 73p
Jack Berry House 2 b.g. ... 77p
King Ottokar (FR) 2 b.c. ... 92p
Lady Amelia 2 b.f. ... 59p
Lady Dauphin (IRE) 2 b.f. ... 69p
Maid For Life 2 b.f. ... 71p
Scorched Breath 2 b.g. ... 74p
Ramsbury 3 b.c. ... 85p
Wise Fox 3 gr.g. ... 54p

JOHN GOSDEN
Albert Finney 2 b.g. ... 74p
Alfaatik 2 b.c. ... 82p
Almashriq (USA) 2 b.c. ... 73P
Ambling (IRE) 2 b.f. ... 79p
Asaatier (USA) 2 b.f. ... 63P
Battle For Glory (USA) 2 b.c. ... 87p
Calyx 2 b.c. ... 120p
Casanova 2 b.c. ... 75P
Cozi Bay 2 gr.f. ... 65p
Daarik (IRE) 2 b.c. ... 86p
Dubai Warrior 2 b.c. ... 104p
Duneflower (IRE) 2 b.f. ... 85p
Entitle 2 b.f. ... 77p
Fabulist 2 b.f. ... 63p
Fanny Logan (IRE) 2 b.f. ... 81p
Forest of Dean 2 b.c. ... 83p
Frisella 2 b.f. ... 82p
Honest Albert 2 ch.c. ... 80p
Humanitarian (USA) 2 ch.c. ... 102p
Kick On 2 b.c. ... 106p
Kimblewick (IRE) 2 b.f. ... 81p

King of Comedy (IRE) 2 b.c. ... 100p
Kosciuszko (IRE) 2 b.c. ... 82p
Lady Lawyer (USA) 2 b.f. ... 74p
Lord North (IRE) 2 b.c. ... 90p
Marhaba Milliar (IRE) 2 b.c. ... 100p
Maximum Effect 2 ch.f. ... 76p
Mehdaayih 2 b.f. ... 83p
Muchly 2 b.c. ... 84p
New King 2 b.c. ... 85p
Oussel Falls 2 b.f. ... 80p
Pianissimo 2 b.c. ... 80p
Private Secretary 2 b.c. ... 89p
Queen of Mayfair 2 b.f. ... 66p
Red Centre (USA) 2 ch.c. ... 78p
She's Got You 2 b.f. ... 84p
Sheriffmuir (USA) 2 b. or br.c. ... 76p
So High 2 ch.c. ... 94p
Sparkle Roll (FR) 2 gr.f. ... 89p
Star Catcher 2 b.f. ... 59p
Stratification (USA) 2 ch.f. ... 78p
Suakin (IRE) 2 b.f. ... 69p
Sucellus 2 b.c. ... 85P
To The Moon 2 b.f. ... 79p
Trapani 2 gr.f. ... 57p
Travel On 2 b.c. ... 87p
Turgenev 2 b.c. ... 106p
Waldstern 2 ch.c. ... 99p
Whimbrel (IRE) 2 gr.f. ... 70p
Anbaa (IRE) 3 b.f. ... 78p
Cassini (IRE) 3 b.c. ... 93p
Corelli (USA) 3 b.c. ... 109p
Derrymore (IRE) 3 b. or br.f. ... 88p
Emblazoned (IRE) 3 b.c. ... 112p
Enbihaar (IRE) 3 b.f. ... 103p
Holy Heart (IRE) 3 b.g. ... 85p
Marechal Ney 3 b.g. ... 87p
Military Law 3 b.g. ... 96p
Mr Marrakech 3 b.c. ... 94p
Mythical Queen 3 b.f. ... 81p
Nordic Passage (IRE) 3 b.c. ... 88p
Star of Bengal 3 b.c. ... 105p
Stream of Stars 3 b.g. ... 92p
Stylehunter 3 ch.c. ... 109p

WILLIAM HAGGAS
Alkaamel 2 b.g. ... 58p
Aplomb (IRE) 2 b.g. ... 85p
Ascended (IRE) 2 gr.f. ... 82p
Coup de Gold (IRE) 2 br.g. ... 75p
Current Option (IRE) 2 b.c. ... 86p
Dalaalaat (IRE) 2 b.c. ... 81p
Dal Horrisgle 2 b.g. ... 82p
Faylaq 2 b.c. ... 76p
Flarepath 2 b.f. ... 80p
Frankellina 2 ch.f. ... 80p
Hidden Message (USA) 2 b. or br.f. ... 90p
Jahbath 2 b.c. ... 95p
Kentucky Kingdom (IRE) 2 b.c. ... 77p
Listen To The Wind (IRE) 2 b.f. ... 87p
Luxor 2 b.c. ... 93p
Maktabba 2 b.f. ... 65p
Montatham 2 gr.c. ... 82p
Mubtasimah 2 b.f. ... 75p
Pablo Escobarr (IRE) 2 b.c. ... 97p
Rainbow Heart (IRE) 2 b.f. ... 92p
Sea of Reality (IRE) 2 b.f. ... 58p

Senza Limiti (IRE) 2 ch.c. ... 95p
Sinjaari (IRE) 2 b.c. ... 66p
Skardu 2 ch.c. ... 96p
Swansdown 2 ch.f. ... 67p
Swiss Air 2 b.f. ... 84p
The Night Watch 2 b.g. ... 90p
Victory Day (IRE) 2 b.g. ... 78p
Wannie Mae (IRE) 2 ch.f. ... 63p
Woods (IRE) 2 b.c. ... 75p
Al Muffrih (IRE) 3 b.g. ... 100p
Big Kitten (USA) 3 ch.g. ... 102p
Hateel (IRE) 3 b.f. ... 68p
Magical Sight 3 b.g. ... 84p
Muneyra 3 b.f. ... 84p
Pretty Baby (IRE) 3 b.f. ... 111p
Young Rascal (FR) 3 b.c. ... 125p

RICHARD HANNON
Bint Soghaan 2 b.f. ... 72p
Canton Queen (IRE) 2 b.f. ... 92p
Dawn Treader (IRE) 2 b.c. ... 78p
Days of Glory (CAN) 2 b.c. ... 84p
Entertaining 2 b.f. ... 59p
Equal Sum 2 b.f. ... 81p
Fox Champion (IRE) 2 b.c. ... 84p
King of Change 2 b.c. ... 80p
Masaru 2 b.c. ... 93p
Motakhayyel 2 b.c. ... 89p
Ouzo 2 b.c. ... 74p
Pesto 2 br.c. ... 85p
Real Smooth (IRE) 2 b.c. ... 87p
Secret Vote (USA) 2 ch.f. ... 57p
Shamkha (IRE) 2 b.f. ... 70p
Sirinapha (IRE) 2 b.c. ... 66p
Star of War (USA) 2 b.f. ... 83p
Urban Icon 2 b.c. ... 99p
Walkinthesand (IRE) 2 b.c. ... 98p
Birthright 3 b.g. ... 79p
Dazzling Diamond 3 ch.f. ... 59p
Rajaam (IRE) 3 b.c. ... 89p

CHARLES HILLS
Alandalos 2 b.f. ... 63p
Breath of Air 2 b.c. ... 97p
Clematis (USA) 2 b. or br.f. ... 80p
Global Quality 2 ch.c. ... 74p
Khaadem (IRE) 2 b.c. ... 110p
Nooshin 2 b.f. ... 80p
Penrhos 2 b.f. ... 79p
Risaala (IRE) 2 b. or br.f. ... 59p
Stagehand 2 b.f. ... 74p
Sundiata 2 b.f. ... 69p
Thakaa (USA) 2 b.f. ... 58P
Vindolanda 2 ch.f. ... 70p
Always A Drama (IRE) 3 b.f. ... 65p

RICHARD HUGHES
Fintas 2 b.c. ... 97p
Little Rock (IRE) 2 gr.g. ... 67p
Carricklane 3 b.f. ... 77p
Napoleonica 3 gr.f. ... 67p

DEAN IVORY
Daddy's Daughter (CAN) 3 b.f. ... 75p
Don't Look Down 3 gr.g. ... 78p
Yimou (IRE) 3 b.g. ... 77p

MARK JOHNSTON

Al Thoorayah (USA) 2 b.c.	72p
Asian Angel (IRE) 2 b.g.	73p
Caplin 2 b.g.	71p
Dame Freya Stark 2 ch.f.	52p
Deep Intrigue 2 gr.c.	96p
Desert Friend (IRE) 2 ch.c.	84p
Fiction Writer (USA) 2 b.c.	75p
Gravistas 2 b.c.	79p
Living Legend (IRE) 2 b.c.	75p
Lord Lamington 2 b.g.	69p
Mind The Crack (IRE) 2 b.g.	81p
Mister Chiang 2 b.c.	80p
Natalie's Joy 2 b.f.	107p
Nayef Road (IRE) 2 ch.c.	100p
New Revenue (IRE) 2 b.f.	70p
Sir Ron Priestley 2 ch.c.	87p
Sky Cross (IRE) 2 b.c.	74p
Themaxwecan (IRE) 2 b.c.	89p
Warning Fire 2 b.f.	70p
West End Charmer (IRE) 2 b.c.	93p
Kwanza 3 b.f.	60p
Matterhorn (IRE) 3 b.c.	105p
Showroom (FR) 3 b.g.	90p

ALAN KING

Chicago Doll 2 ch.f.	73p
Chicago Guy 2 ch.c.	57p
Green Etoile 2 ch.g.	58p
Hummdinger (FR) 2 ch.g.	61p
Peckinpah (IRE) 2 ch.g.	74p
Princesse Mathilde 2 gr.f.	72p
The Olympian (IRE) 2 ch.g.	87p
Nebuchadnezzar (FR) 3 b.g.	78p

SYLVESTER KIRK

Benny And The Jets (IRE) 2 ch.g.	76p
Irene May (IRE) 2 b.f.	80p

DAVID LANIGAN

Burning Topic (GER) 2 b.f.	78P
Irish Art (IRE) 2 b.g.	72p
Malika I Jahan (FR) 2 b.f.	72p
Millions Memories 2 b.g.	86p
Sunset Flash (IRE) 2 b.f.	82p

MARTYN MEADE

Airwaves 2 b.f.	74p
Cadre du Noir (USA) 2 b.c.	79p
Crackling (IRE) 2 b.c.	93p
Engrossed (IRE) 2 ch.f.	73p
King Ademar (USA) 2 b. or br.c.	85p
Lyzbeth (FR) 2 b.f.	72p
Monogamy 2 br. or gr.f.	68p
Numero Uno 2 b.c.	68p
Palladium 2 b.c.	76p
Technician (IRE) 2 gr.c.	75p

BRIAN MEEHAN

Colonel Slade (IRE) 2 b.c.	57p
Dominus (IRE) 2 ch.c.	62p
Dubai Instinct 2 b.c.	70p
Jilbaab 2 b.c.	68p
Kaloor 2 b.c.	85p

DAVID MENUISIER

Edmond Dantes (IRE) 2 gr.c.	68p
Migration (IRE) 2 b.c.	73p
Atalanta's Boy 3 b.c.	66p

HUGHIE MORRISON

Craster (IRE) 2 b.c.	88p
Lieutenant Conde 2 b.g.	61p
Mums Hope 2 gr.f.	78p
Tartlette 2 b.f.	50p
Our Nelson 3 b.g.	82p

AIDAN O'BRIEN, IRELAND

Albuquerque (IRE) 2 b.c.	87p
Cape of Good Hope (IRE) 2 b.c.	103p
Chablis (IRE) 2 b.f.	85p
Circus Maximus (IRE) 2 b.c.	112p
Constantinople (IRE) 2 b.c.	92p
Fleeting (IRE) 2 b.f.	107p
Frosty (IRE) 2 gr.f.	89p
Gentile Bellini 2 b.c.	90p
Il Paradiso (USA) 2 ch.c.	95p
Japan 2 b.c.	113p
Magna Grecia (IRE) 2 b.c.	116p
Mount Everest (IRE) 2 b.c.	111p
Norway (IRE) 2 ch.c.	107p
Old Glory (IRE) 2 b.c.	101p
Pink Dogwood (IRE) 2 br.f.	100p
Ten Sovereigns (IRE) 2 b.c.	120p
Turnberry Isle (IRE) 2 b.c.	95p

JOSEPH PATRICK O'BRIEN, IRELAND

Iridessa (IRE) 2 b.f.	113p
King's Field (IRE) 3 b.c.	113p
Sir Erec (IRE) 3 b.c.	119p

DAVID O'MEARA

Gylo (IRE) 2 b.g.	69p
Leodis Dream (IRE) 2 b.g.	86p
Lincoln Tale (IRE) 2 b.f.	56p
Very Dainty (IRE) 2 b.f.	67p
Makawee (IRE) 3 b.f.	77p

HUGO PALMER

Artois 2 b.c.	92p
Birdcage Walk 2 b.f.	57p
Debbonair (IRE) 2 b.g.	72p
Gold Fleece 2 b.f.	53p
Hostess 2 b.f.	84p
Mina Vagante 2 b.f.	60p
Power of States (IRE) 2 b.c.	80p
Set Piece 2 b.c.	86p
Wall of Sapphire (IRE) 2 b.f.	68p
Collide 3 b.c.	111p
Referee 3 b.g.	87p
Sudona 3 b.f.	82p

SIR MARK PRESCOTT BT

Albanita 2 gr.f.	80p
All Points West 2 b.g.	84p
Alma Linda 2 gr.f.	60p
Autonomy 2 b.g.	54p
Brassica (IRE) 2 b.f.	79p
Buckman Tavern (FR) 2 b.g.	81p
Chancer 2 b.g.	58p
Eve Harrington (USA) 2 b.f.	68p
Hydroplane (IRE) 2 b.g.	54p
Klass Action (IRE) 2 b.f.	79p
Grey Spirit (IRE) 3 gr.g.	88p
Timoshenko 3 ch.g.	90p
Elysees Palace 4 b.g.	85p

KEVIN RYAN

Arogo 2 b.g.	62p
Captain Combat (FR) 2 ch.c.	65p
Conga 2 ch.f.	81p
Dream Chick (IRE) 2 br.f.	56p
East 2 ch.f.	106p
Hello Youmzain (FR) 2 b.c.	112p
Last Empire 2 b.f.	60p
Magical Spirit (IRE) 2 ch.g.	79p
Secret Venture 2 b.c.	90p
Shaqwar 2 ch.f.	63p
Bielsa (IRE) 3 b.c.	63p

GEORGE SCOTT

Aadya 2 b.f.	69p
Alabama Dreaming 2 gr.f.	67p
Lyndon B (IRE) 2 b.c.	82p
Merge (IRE) 2 b.g.	56p
Advanced Virgo (IRE) 3 b.g.	78p
Bigshotte 3 b.g.	56p

DAVID SIMCOCK

Alemagna 2 b.f.	79p
Bubbelah (IRE) 2 b.g.	50p
Delachance 2 b.f.	54p
Desert Land (IRE) 2 b.c.	80p
Durston 2 ch.c.	82p
Narrative (IRE) 2 b.f.	72p
Omnivega (IRE) 2 b.f.	78p
Poetic Era 2 b.f.	68p
Prejudice 2 ch.c.	88p
Raakib Alhawa (IRE) 2 b.c.	99p
Red Bunting (IRE) 2 b.f.	70p
Shamameya (IRE) 2 ch.f.	67p
Spanish Mission (USA) 2 b.c.	96p
Universal Order 2 ch.c.	88p
Vexed 2 b.g.	79p
Woven 2 ch.c.	90p
Birch Grove (IRE) 3 b.f.	78p
Imperial Court (IRE) 3 b.g.	83p
Miss Latin (IRE) 3 b.f.	86p
Mugatoo (IRE) 3 b.g.	86p
Supernova 3 b.c.	101p
Tranquil Storm (IRE) 3 b.f.	59p

SIR MICHAEL STOUTE

Accommodate (IRE) 2 b.f.	81p
Alhaazm 2 b.c.	74p
Alignak 2 b.c.	67p
Almania (IRE) 2 b.c.	90p
Anna of Lorraine 2 b.f.	74p
Calculation 2 br.c.	71p
Clerisy 2 b.f.	69p
Deal A Dollar 2 b.c.	91p
Derevo 2 b.c.	75p
El Picador (IRE) 2 b.c.	70p
Felix 2 ch.c.	87p
Gracefully Done (IRE) 2 ch.f.	76p
Hawthorn Rose 2 ch.f.	72p
Honfleur (IRE) 2 ch.f.	61p
Laafy (USA) 2 b.c.	86p
Loolwah (IRE) 2 gr.f.	78p
Madeeh 2 b.c.	71p
Mokammal 2 b.c.	87p
Mubakker (USA) 2 gr.c.	102p

Mulan (IRE) 2 b.f.	75p
Nantucket (IRE) 2 b.f.	61p
Neon Sea (FR) 2 b.f.	69p
Romola 2 b.f.	85p
Sangarius 2 b.c.	107p
Solid Stone (IRE) 2 br.c.	87p
Song Without End (IRE) 2 b.c.	66P
Sovereign Grant 2 b.c.	89p
Top Top (IRE) 2 b.c.	76p
Vivionn 2 ch.f.	84p
Baritone (IRE) 3 b.g.	91p
Crystal King 3 ch.g.	93p
Ledham (IRE) 3 b.c.	98p
Rawdaa 3 b.f.	105p
Shareef Star 3 b.c.	87p
Adamant (GER) 4 gr.g.	108p

SAEED BIN SUROOR

Autumn Leaf (IRE) 2 b.f.	68P
Diamond Oasis 2 ch.f.	76p
Dubai Blue (USA) 2 b.f.	90p
Dubai Discovery (USA) 2 b. or br.f.	75p
Dubai Ice (USA) 2 ch.f.	68p
Dubai Icon 2 b.c.	85p
Dubai Legacy (USA) 2 ch.c.	93p
Dubai Luxury 2 b.f.	60p
Falathaat (USA) 2 ch.f.	78p
Global Heat (IRE) 2 b.g.	87p
Magic Image 2 ch.f.	79p
Mawahib (IRE) 2 ch.f.	79p
Najib (IRE) 2 b.g.	58p
Promise of Success 2 b.f.	81p
Royal Marine (IRE) 2 b.c.	113p
Royal Meeting (IRE) 2 b.c.	114p
Shoot For Gold 2 b.c.	93p
Silent Hunter 2 b.c.	86p
Swift Rose (IRE) 2 b.f.	87p
Winter Sky (IRE) 2 b.f.	55p
Beauvais (IRE) 3 ch.c.	88p
Cantiniere (USA) 3 b.f.	88p
Desert Fire (IRE) 3 b.c.	99p
Jalaad (IRE) 3 b.g.	88p
Laieth 3 b.g.	96p
Major Partnership (IRE) 3 gr.c.	110p
Military Band 3 ch.c.	84p
National Army 3 b.c.	93p
Racing Country (IRE) 3 b.g.	103p
Reaction Time 3 b.c.	83p
Welsh Lord 3 gr.g.	100p
Dayking 4 b.h.	104p
Glassy Waters (USA) 4 ch.h.	104p
Silver River 4 gr.g.	99p

JAMES TATE

Attainment 2 ch.c.	83p
Cape Victory (IRE) 2 b.c.	68p
Evolutionary (IRE) 2 b.f.	72p
Fields of Athenry (USA) 2 b.c.	82p
Intuitive (IRE) 2 b.c.	90p
Local History 2 b.f.	72p
Moonlit Sea 2 b.g.	72p
Name The Wind 2 b.c.	95p
The Met 2 b.c.	69p
Top Rank (IRE) 2 gr.c.	83p
Astonished (IRE) 3 ch.f.	87p
Leap of Faith 3 ch.c.	58p

MARCUS TREGONING

Mohaather 2 b.c.	110p
Strindberg 2 b.c.	67p
Freckles 3 ch.f.	54p
Power of Darkness 3 b.g.	96p

ROGER VARIAN

Apparate 2 b.c.	86p
Backstreet Girl (IRE) 2 b.f.	64p
Bayroot (IRE) 2 b.c.	90p
Daring Venture (IRE) 2 b.f.	68p
Dashed 2 b.f.	79p
Elamirr (IRE) 2 b.c.	81p
Emirates Knight (IRE) 2 b.c.	80p
Enough Already 2 b.g.	85p
Fabriano (GER) 2 b.c.	74p
Gleeful 2 b.f.	76p
Ideological (IRE) 2 b.f.	85p
Jaleel 2 b.c.	76p
Just My Type 2 ch.f.	73p
Khuzaam (USA) 2 ch.c.	93p
Lastochka 2 ch.f.	78p
Lehoogg 2 ch.c.	79p
Lilligram 2 b.f.	57p
Lufricia 2 b.f.	71p
Mackaar (IRE) 2 b.c.	81p
Manorah (IRE) 2 b.f.	78p
Mawakib 2 b.c.	75p
Monsieur Noir 2 b.c.	90p
Moqtarreb 2 b.c.	67p

Moraawed 2 b.g.	90p
Mosakhar 2 b.c.	73p
Motalaqqy (IRE) 2 b.c.	84p
Motawaj 2 b.c.	75p
Mot Juste (USA) 2 b.f.	102p
Nabbeyl (IRE) 2 b.c.	83p
Nausha 2 b.f.	86P
Nearooz 2 b.f.	88p
Prince Eiji 2 ch.c.	100p
Qabala (USA) 2 b.f.	93p
Red Desert (IRE) 2 b.g.	59p
Regal Banner 2 ch.f.	72p
Revolutionise (IRE) 2 gr.c.	65p
San Donato (IRE) 2 b.c.	115p
Shagalla 2 b.f.	78p
Surfman 2 b.c.	87p
Tammooz 2 b.c.	64p
Tauteke 2 b.f.	92p
Turjomaan (USA) 2 b. or br.c.	97p
Act of Bravery 3 b.c.	78p
Canvassed (IRE) 3 b.g.	84p
Ekanse (IRE) 3 b.g.	61p
Hermosita 3 b.f.	83p
Howman (IRE) 3 b.g.	88p
Imaginative (IRE) 3 b.g.	88p
Lady Momoka (IRE) 3 b.f.	74p
Monteja 3 b.f.	81p
Narynkol 3 ch.g.	96p

Qazyna (IRE) 3 b.f.	105p
Sparkling Surf 3 ch.f.	53p
Ta Allak 3 ch.c.	83p
Willie John 3 b.c.	99p
Fujaira Prince (IRE) 4 gr. or ro.g.	86p

ED VAUGHAN

Al Battar (IRE) 2 b.c.	72P
Ardiente 2 b.f.	85p
Dame Malliot 2 b.f.	83p
Magic J (USA) 2 ch.c.	96p
Desert Wind (IRE) 3 b.c.	103p
Nasee 3 b.c.	62p

ED WALKER

Baba Ghanouj (IRE) 2 b.f.	84p
Came From The Dark (IRE) 2 gr.c.	79p
Cap Francais 2 b.c.	94p
Dreamweaver (IRE) 2 b.g.	65p
Gallic 2 b.f.	87p
Ginistrelli (IRE) 2 b.c.	84p
I'm Freezing (IRE) 2 b.f.	65p
Shug 2 b.g.	58p
Akbar Shah (IRE) 3 b.g.	94p
Capriolette (IRE) 3 b.f.	75p
Caradoc (IRE) 3 b.g.	92p
Clooney 3 b.g.	73p
Singing Sheriff 3 b.g.	63p
Tinos (GER) 4 b.g.	78p

CHRIS WALL

Solfeggio (IRE) 2 br.f.	72p
Follow Intello (IRE) 3 b.g.	77p
Trade Talks 3 b.g.	84p

ARCHIE WATSON

Gatria 2 ch.f.	65p
Harvey Dent 2 ch.g.	82p
Perfect Grace 2 b.f.	62p
Surrey Breeze (IRE) 2 b.c.	55p
Victoriano (IRE) 2 b.g.	57p
Zaula 2 gr.f.	71p

D. K. WELD, IRELAND

Masaff (IRE) 2 ch.c.	108p
Rakan 2 b.c.	95p
Tarnawa (IRE) 2 ch.f.	93p
Zuenoon (IRE) 2 gr.c.	98p
Flavius (USA) 3 b.c.	113p

IAN WILLIAMS

Gabrial The Giant (IRE) 2 b.g.	66p
Matewan (IRE) 3 b.g.	80p

STUART WILLIAMS

Marronnier (IRE) 2 ch.g.	86p
No Trouble (IRE) 2 b.g.	57p
Rhythmic Intent (IRE) 2 ch.c.	78p
Sarsaparilla Kit 2 b.f.	51p
Broughton Excels 3 b.g.	67p
Department of War (IRE) 3 ch.c.	93p

TRAINERS FOR COURSES

The following statistics show the most successful trainers over the past five seasons at each of the courses that stage Flat racing in England, Scotland and Wales. Impact Value is expressed as a factor of a trainer's number of winners compared to those expected to occur by chance. Market Value is expressed as the factor by which the % chance of an Industry Starting Price exceeds random, as implied by field size. For example, a horse that is shorter than 3/1 in a 4-runner field will have a market value above 1.

ASCOT

Trainer	Wins	Runs	Strike Rate	% Rivals Beaten	P/L	Run To Form %	Impact Value	Market Value
John Gosden	44	259	16.99%	60.50	-15.46	40.10	1.90	1.79
Aidan O'Brien, Ireland	29	206	14.08%	59.06	-22.68	41.75	1.65	2.01
Richard Hannon	26	350	7.43%	48.58	-173.70	22.01	0.82	1.16
William Haggas	25	188	13.30%	56.69	-40.94	29.96	1.53	1.69
Sir Michael Stoute	22	157	14.01%	61.43	-3.93	39.49	1.40	1.86
Charlie Appleby	22	162	13.58%	58.38	-21.85	33.13	1.56	1.71
Mark Johnston	22	251	8.76%	48.65	-88.38	26.29	1.00	1.09
Roger Varian	17	134	12.69%	53.04	-25.27	27.01	1.51	1.60
Saeed bin Suroor	14	106	13.21%	51.96	-24.79	32.08	1.62	1.52
Andrew Balding	14	176	7.95%	48.58	-77.00	27.27	0.90	1.12

AYR

Trainer	Wins	Runs	Strike Rate	% Rivals Beaten	P/L	Run To Form %	Impact Value	Market Value
Keith Dalgleish	59	498	11.85%	51.59	-11.23	20.66	1.07	1.10
Jim Goldie	58	640	9.06%	49.79	-126.54	16.58	0.82	1.01
Richard Fahey	35	382	9.16%	54.16	-145.99	19.63	0.89	1.44
Michael Dods	34	278	12.23%	57.82	-0.88	22.71	1.16	1.34
David O'Meara	34	212	16.04%	53.24	-25.88	21.70	1.48	1.49
K. R. Burke	25	128	19.53%	55.94	-9.14	30.47	1.71	1.46
Ruth Carr	24	184	13.04%	49.21	-4.55	16.48	1.19	1.18
Linda Perratt	23	348	6.61%	42.39	-111.25	13.07	0.64	0.68
Iain Jardine	21	187	11.23%	45.46	-43.25	16.58	1.02	1.07
R. Mike Smith	19	157	12.10%	48.48	54.50	19.11	1.08	1.04

BATH

Trainer	Wins	Runs	Strike Rate	% Rivals Beaten	P/L	Run To Form %	Impact Value	Market Value
Malcolm Saunders	31	150	20.67%	56.02	21.91	28.39	1.61	1.31
Richard Hannon	28	171	16.37%	57.56	-49.21	29.85	1.21	1.59
Mick Channon	27	157	17.20%	55.91	-18.30	28.18	1.33	1.43
Clive Cox	22	114	19.30%	60.44	-24.58	35.67	1.43	1.84
Charles Hills	21	89	23.60%	64.73	15.41	38.91	1.65	1.48
Mark Johnston	18	82	21.95%	58.93	-16.96	42.36	1.32	1.50
Rod Millman	18	104	17.31%	53.49	54.88	30.38	1.42	1.20
Roger Charlton	17	52	32.69%	70.73	18.44	41.47	2.31	2.14
Tony Carroll	17	144	11.81%	49.37	-13.42	19.85	1.12	1.06
Ronald Harris	17	178	9.55%	46.42	-42.75	18.75	0.77	0.84

BEVERLEY

Trainer	Wins	Runs	Strike Rate	% Rivals Beaten	P/L	Run To Form %	Impact Value	Market Value
Richard Fahey	54	366	14.75%	59.14	-122.78	30.16	1.27	1.56
Mark Johnston	51	273	18.68%	57.17	-45.80	33.25	1.39	1.67
David O'Meara	40	262	15.27%	57.68	-8.67	27.66	1.30	1.46
Tim Easterby	38	342	11.11%	49.56	-125.58	22.64	1.00	1.17
Kevin Ryan	20	178	11.24%	55.71	-8.67	29.83	1.03	1.37
Brian Ellison	17	148	11.49%	48.24	-35.06	21.45	1.03	0.99
Richard Guest	15	79	18.99%	51.37	40.75	26.58	1.94	1.16
Les Eyre	15	113	13.27%	52.27	-10.95	20.75	1.30	1.27
Ollie Pears	15	138	10.87%	50.95	43.25	21.30	1.03	0.94
Michael Dods	15	77	19.48%	58.06	3.25	31.13	1.85	1.60

BRIGHTON

Trainer	Wins	Runs	Strike Rate	% Rivals Beaten	P/L	Run To Form %	Impact Value	Market Value
Richard Hannon	38	153	24.84%	58.39	34.02	34.73	1.72	1.51
Tony Carroll	35	208	16.83%	57.80	0.64	24.40	1.38	1.30
Gary Moore	34	209	16.27%	53.75	21.10	21.96	1.29	1.25
John Bridger	21	151	13.91%	55.45	-6.54	19.21	1.15	1.09
John Gallagher	21	103	20.39%	57.05	57.25	30.29	1.47	1.19
Mick Channon	20	147	13.61%	57.70	11.45	26.03	1.02	1.25
Richard Hughes	20	78	25.64%	62.53	10.57	37.18	1.72	1.43
Eve Johnson Houghton	18	86	20.93%	61.14	-6.96	32.99	1.57	1.41
Mark Johnston	16	92	17.39%	51.66	-24.53	29.64	1.14	1.66
Philip Hide	15	80	18.75%	60.57	-8.81	29.64	1.37	1.61

CARLISLE

Trainer	Wins	Runs	Strike Rate	% Rivals Beaten	P/L	Run To Form %	Impact Value	Market Value
Keith Dalgleish	34	261	13.03%	49.96	-55.83	22.74	1.09	1.20
Richard Fahey	31	260	11.92%	57.84	-91.80	27.78	0.98	1.39
Mark Johnston	24	144	16.67%	56.80	-32.67	29.14	1.21	1.53
Tim Easterby	24	234	10.26%	51.67	-67.03	21.25	0.89	1.16
K. R. Burke	24	108	22.22%	60.38	47.95	35.38	1.76	1.36
Kevin Ryan	16	105	15.24%	60.64	-25.95	29.93	1.35	1.35
Michael Dods	15	129	11.63%	56.66	-47.63	27.06	1.05	1.38
Brian Ellison	10	74	13.51%	53.59	-23.81	17.76	1.22	1.28
Ann Duffield	10	74	13.51%	46.16	-3.02	24.70	1.11	0.95
Bryan Smart	8	67	11.94%	51.28	-1.50	21.97	1.03	1.17

CATTERICK BRIDGE

Trainer	Wins	Runs	Strike Rate	% Rivals Beaten	P/L	Run To Form %	Impact Value	Market Value
Richard Fahey	42	223	18.83%	57.97	-12.58	27.75	1.54	1.48
John Quinn	29	168	17.26%	58.05	10.71	25.48	1.47	1.34
Mark Johnston	27	152	17.76%	47.30	-39.75	23.37	1.30	1.58
Tim Easterby	24	230	10.43%	54.09	-59.65	20.32	0.95	1.11
David O'Meara	23	193	11.92%	55.08	-79.93	18.90	1.05	1.48
Ruth Carr	20	158	12.66%	55.68	-40.00	16.56	1.26	1.29
Keith Dalgleish	18	101	17.82%	52.56	34.83	28.02	1.53	1.21
Brian Ellison	15	102	14.71%	58.17	-21.60	22.55	1.24	1.35
Michael Bell	14	32	43.75%	71.35	27.69	50.00	3.55	2.29
Michael Easterby	14	145	9.66%	49.24	-49.38	17.98	0.93	0.94

CHELMSFORD CITY (AW)

Trainer	Wins	Runs	Strike Rate	% Rivals Beaten	P/L	Run To Form %	Impact Value	Market Value
Mark Johnston	59	370	15.95%	51.34	-80.40	30.10	1.21	1.33
David Simcock	45	221	20.36%	57.11	20.59	31.49	1.53	1.33
Saeed bin Suroor	44	142	30.99%	70.01	-8.63	43.99	2.46	2.58
Stuart Williams	41	267	15.36%	57.09	0.88	24.06	1.33	1.33
William Haggas	41	162	25.31%	65.42	-12.08	43.48	2.06	2.38
John Gosden	40	174	22.99%	66.40	-41.43	42.12	1.81	2.28
Marco Botti	40	278	14.39%	57.61	-1.10	32.83	1.15	1.41
Michael Appleby	39	396	9.85%	48.00	-152.88	16.28	0.82	1.09
Derek Shaw	37	279	13.26%	46.89	4.29	19.14	1.14	0.94
Chris Dwyer	33	204	16.18%	52.87	21.04	23.64	1.29	1.17

CHEPSTOW

Trainer	Wins	Runs	Strike Rate	% Rivals Beaten	P/L	Run To Form %	Impact Value	Market Value
Richard Hannon	27	149	18.12%	55.40	-42.96	28.37	1.42	1.59
David Evans	26	217	11.98%	52.94	-7.95	21.98	0.98	1.06
Andrew Balding	21	109	19.27%	59.46	-9.08	31.77	1.51	1.78
Ralph Beckett	18	60	30.00%	63.09	-7.08	43.21	2.18	2.23
John O'Shea	17	130	13.08%	47.69	1.33	20.33	1.04	0.96
Ed de Giles	17	62	27.42%	58.86	57.25	34.10	2.22	1.24
Eve Johnson Houghton	16	64	25.00%	65.38	7.68	41.08	1.95	1.50
Ronald Harris	14	167	8.38%	45.29	-36.90	14.55	0.76	0.83
Bernard Llewellyn	13	110	11.82%	48.19	6.67	21.29	0.96	0.97
Mick Channon	13	91	14.29%	55.22	-2.46	23.25	1.21	1.45

CHESTER

Trainer	Wins	Runs	Strike Rate	% Rivals Beaten	P/L	Run To Form %	Impact Value	Market Value
Richard Fahey	64	517	12.38%	55.10	-93.84	21.81	1.08	1.32
Andrew Balding	45	183	24.59%	61.76	76.27	41.20	1.91	1.52
Mark Johnston	40	263	15.21%	52.99	-73.06	26.37	1.18	1.43
Tom Dascombe	38	299	12.71%	50.16	-112.59	25.47	1.05	1.21
Tim Easterby	18	130	13.85%	48.99	-3.75	20.77	1.25	1.12
Kevin Ryan	15	77	19.48%	56.00	8.91	28.57	1.74	1.35
Richard Hannon	15	94	15.96%	58.14	-15.86	31.91	1.20	1.44
William Haggas	12	40	30.00%	66.72	-3.77	40.00	2.12	2.11
Aidan O'Brien, Ireland	12	34	35.29%	67.59	-1.33	69.70	2.57	2.20
Brian Ellison	10	71	14.08%	50.71	-3.50	23.94	1.30	1.28

DONCASTER

Trainer	Wins	Runs	Strike Rate	% Rivals Beaten	P/L	Run To Form %	Impact Value	Market Value
Richard Fahey	44	462	9.52%	52.67	-84.74	20.27	1.00	1.26
Richard Hannon	39	309	12.62%	55.48	-27.52	32.55	1.13	1.45
Roger Varian	38	156	24.36%	68.89	29.11	46.20	2.23	2.15
John Gosden	28	160	17.50%	63.10	-56.00	41.79	1.65	2.26
Sir Michael Stoute	26	77	33.77%	70.74	49.82	55.52	2.93	2.32
Mark Johnston	25	176	14.20%	47.53	-36.35	25.90	1.15	1.20
Charlie Appleby	23	115	20.00%	62.06	-9.18	45.43	1.75	1.93
David O'Meara	23	261	8.81%	52.22	-95.59	19.82	0.93	1.29
William Haggas	21	112	18.75%	65.62	-27.42	36.58	1.67	2.04
Saeed bin Suroor	21	68	30.88%	64.91	7.47	44.12	2.47	2.37

TRAINERS FOR COURSES

EPSOM

Trainer	Wins	Runs	Strike Rate	% Rivals Beaten	P/L	Run To Form %	Impact Value	Market Value
Mark Johnston	23	138	16.67%	50.09	-26.07	23.19	1.31	1.41
Mick Channon	15	65	23.08%	53.88	26.03	33.85	1.76	1.01
John Gosden	14	50	28.00%	65.48	-2.54	52.00	2.28	2.11
Richard Fahey	13	113	11.50%	52.50	-19.38	17.70	1.01	1.22
Andrew Balding	13	105	12.38%	59.59	-0.29	26.16	1.00	1.58
Richard Hannon	12	91	13.19%	51.89	-33.54	27.21	0.96	1.23
Roger Varian	10	37	27.03%	65.76	8.38	50.39	2.08	1.85
Ralph Beckett	9	52	17.31%	53.62	-9.43	31.46	1.39	1.28
George Baker	9	45	20.00%	50.19	37.75	24.44	1.80	1.14
Eve Johnson Houghton	9	41	21.95%	56.46	9.48	29.62	1.78	1.19

FFOS LAS

Trainer	Wins	Runs	Strike Rate	% Rivals Beaten	P/L	Run To Form %	Impact Value	Market Value
David Evans	19	150	12.67%	49.34	35.25	22.94	0.91	0.97
Andrew Balding	16	62	25.81%	64.47	42.52	50.04	1.71	1.43
Rod Millman	10	54	18.52%	49.21	-10.00	24.07	1.33	1.19
William Muir	9	44	20.45%	51.60	13.75	29.22	1.37	1.06
Richard Hannon	8	46	17.39%	57.89	-12.50	36.96	1.26	1.52
Roger Charlton	7	27	25.93%	65.63	29.48	31.31	1.92	2.26
Charles Hills	5	26	19.23%	59.59	10.16	35.58	1.42	1.24
Tony Carroll	5	35	14.29%	55.36	-2.00	20.00	1.28	1.14
Hughie Morrison	5	25	20.00%	55.02	0.00	36.00	1.49	1.30
Richard Hughes	5	27	18.52%	64.48	8.18	44.44	1.36	1.50

GOODWOOD

Trainer	Wins	Runs	Strike Rate	% Rivals Beaten	P/L	Run To Form %	Impact Value	Market Value
Mark Johnston	48	309	15.53%	55.43	68.83	31.48	1.53	1.37
Richard Hannon	44	409	10.76%	51.21	-138.60	25.66	0.98	1.29
Mick Channon	27	216	12.50%	48.92	-11.54	22.46	1.16	1.01
Sir Michael Stoute	24	120	20.00%	62.62	-30.88	40.83	1.64	1.81
William Haggas	23	112	20.54%	61.40	-12.35	37.50	1.97	1.86
Charlie Appleby	22	106	20.75%	57.85	-1.84	33.38	1.94	1.84
John Gosden	22	111	19.82%	58.00	-26.17	48.14	1.48	1.82
Andrew Balding	19	169	11.24%	53.09	-55.01	30.42	1.06	1.26
David Simcock	17	124	13.71%	50.43	17.50	24.19	1.18	1.18
Gary Moore	14	110	12.73%	40.39	106.21	22.02	1.24	0.84

HAMILTON

Trainer	Wins	Runs	Strike Rate	% Rivals Beaten	P/L	Run To Form %	Impact Value	Market Value
Keith Dalgleish	62	482	12.86%	50.54	-79.41	22.29	1.02	1.14
Mark Johnston	41	217	18.89%	56.11	-41.45	33.06	1.36	1.48
Richard Fahey	37	282	13.12%	52.25	-85.63	24.04	0.98	1.28
Kevin Ryan	33	154	21.43%	55.22	15.71	34.35	1.68	1.30
David O'Meara	28	143	19.58%	57.01	-29.28	25.87	1.44	1.53
John Patrick Shanahan, Ire	20	104	19.23%	56.29	-1.23	31.98	1.48	1.41
Tim Easterby	20	102	19.61%	61.91	40.65	26.47	1.69	1.47
Jim Goldie	20	197	10.15%	47.62	-29.35	16.77	0.85	1.00
Iain Jardine	19	154	12.34%	48.93	30.55	20.40	1.00	1.04
Michael Dods	14	75	18.67%	58.74	-11.18	29.70	1.57	1.46

HAYDOCK PARK

Trainer	Wins	Runs	Strike Rate	% Rivals Beaten	P/L	Run To Form %	Impact Value	Market Value
Tom Dascombe	64	364	17.58%	55.08	224.90	31.10	1.45	1.29
Mark Johnston	39	248	15.73%	53.58	-10.80	30.38	1.23	1.21
William Haggas	35	122	28.69%	66.61	3.71	52.14	2.38	2.15
Richard Fahey	35	373	9.38%	50.31	-156.89	19.29	0.86	1.07
John Gosden	30	100	30.00%	70.30	46.60	52.72	2.46	2.02
David O'Meara	29	248	11.69%	48.35	15.47	20.66	1.04	1.17
Richard Hannon	24	220	10.91%	52.26	-66.06	27.30	0.89	1.31
K. R. Burke	22	204	10.78%	47.25	-37.42	22.22	0.94	1.05
Tim Easterby	21	222	9.46%	46.35	-23.00	15.84	0.87	0.93
Hugo Palmer	18	59	30.51%	64.20	81.20	51.67	2.60	1.72

KEMPTON PARK (AW)

Trainer	Wins	Runs	Strike Rate	% Rivals Beaten	P/L	Run To Form %	Impact Value	Market Value
John Gosden	77	310	24.84%	66.90	12.17	43.67	2.41	2.46
Richard Hannon	74	656	11.28%	55.26	-199.42	29.83	1.05	1.36
Charlie Appleby	66	221	29.86%	68.84	-2.53	48.85	2.60	2.66
James Fanshawe	60	326	18.40%	65.75	-45.80	36.90	1.83	1.83
Ralph Beckett	50	305	16.39%	59.34	23.45	36.12	1.59	1.81
Roger Varian	46	226	20.35%	67.06	-28.45	41.85	2.07	2.08
Andrew Balding	45	364	12.36%	56.39	-97.90	26.47	1.16	1.51
Saeed bin Suroor	42	181	23.20%	71.48	-24.41	45.71	2.21	2.92
Tony Carroll	40	509	7.86%	48.59	-230.25	16.31	0.82	1.08
Clive Cox	36	245	14.69%	58.25	16.04	29.39	1.46	1.46

LEICESTER

Trainer	Wins	Runs	Strike Rate	% Rivals Beaten	P/L	Run To Form %	Impact Value	Market Value
Richard Fahey	32	172	18.60%	57.05	8.80	27.04	1.57	1.48
Richard Hannon	31	212	14.62%	54.23	-49.35	31.28	1.21	1.31
Mark Johnston	29	143	20.28%	58.17	-14.61	34.78	1.48	1.34
Mick Channon	20	95	21.05%	58.30	28.18	29.12	1.70	1.45
Sir Michael Stoute	19	82	23.17%	62.19	-16.83	48.57	1.95	2.00
Charles Hills	19	87	21.84%	60.01	14.60	38.95	1.86	1.53
Roger Varian	15	85	17.65%	56.12	-23.57	28.57	1.36	1.88
David Evans	14	140	10.00%	51.44	-27.50	20.29	0.86	1.00
David O'Meara	12	84	14.29%	52.23	-33.70	22.62	1.14	1.42
Saeed bin Suroor	12	43	27.91%	65.38	0.48	42.51	2.16	2.52

LINGFIELD PARK (AW)

Trainer	Wins	Runs	Strike Rate	% Rivals Beaten	P/L	Run To Form %	Impact Value	Market Value
Richard Hannon	73	412	17.72%	56.21	2.99	31.94	1.41	1.44
Mark Johnston	64	352	18.18%	52.64	-39.94	31.13	1.34	1.45
Charlie Appleby	52	164	31.71%	68.83	6.83	46.51	2.42	2.56
John Gosden	49	242	20.25%	64.43	-58.54	38.60	1.69	2.30
Andrew Balding	45	283	15.90%	53.51	-63.48	28.26	1.32	1.40
William Haggas	42	153	27.45%	69.25	0.68	40.52	2.32	2.48
David Evans	42	366	11.48%	50.64	-153.09	18.67	0.95	1.28
Ralph Beckett	40	173	23.12%	58.15	-4.28	37.78	1.89	1.85
Simon Dow	36	280	12.86%	52.71	0.77	25.08	1.09	1.12
Gary Moore	34	316	10.76%	47.74	-109.05	18.91	0.92	1.24

LINGFIELD PARK (TURF)

Trainer	Wins	Runs	Strike Rate	% Rivals Beaten	P/L	Run To Form %	Impact Value	Market Value
Richard Hannon	25	148	16.89%	60.34	-12.51	34.96	1.30	1.64
William Haggas	24	53	45.28%	73.25	40.96	63.51	3.37	2.38
John Bridger	16	119	13.45%	52.74	40.13	20.17	1.24	1.04
Jim Boyle	14	58	24.14%	53.32	49.50	31.61	2.02	1.03
Andrew Balding	14	57	24.56%	57.37	1.00	39.32	1.83	1.76
Roger Varian	11	46	23.91%	70.81	-9.22	51.23	1.91	2.44
Gary Moore	11	86	12.79%	49.30	-18.25	25.72	0.99	1.01
David Evans	10	71	14.08%	58.57	1.78	29.07	1.15	1.23
Mick Channon	10	103	9.71%	56.60	-38.04	23.17	0.75	1.29
Patrick Chamings	9	32	28.13%	63.86	36.33	37.50	2.19	1.06

MUSSELBURGH

Trainer	Wins	Runs	Strike Rate	% Rivals Beaten	P/L	Run To Form %	Impact Value	Market Value
Keith Dalgleish	51	415	12.29%	48.64	-91.69	23.02	0.95	1.11
Mark Johnston	50	249	20.08%	58.30	-5.34	35.32	1.40	1.54
Richard Fahey	45	242	18.60%	59.04	59.30	34.08	1.40	1.39
Jim Goldie	29	324	8.95%	45.85	-72.09	15.00	0.76	0.94
Kevin Ryan	22	105	20.95%	55.89	22.63	28.57	1.64	1.35
David O'Meara	20	146	13.70%	55.31	-53.15	25.04	1.04	1.43
Tim Easterby	18	155	11.61%	50.51	-36.55	24.52	0.98	1.25
Iain Jardine	17	167	10.18%	50.51	-81.98	24.87	0.78	1.05
Linda Perratt	15	226	6.64%	41.19	-43.50	15.56	0.57	0.65
Rebecca Bastiman	15	83	18.07%	64.02	11.25	29.11	1.58	1.24

NEWBURY

Trainer	Wins	Runs	Strike Rate	% Rivals Beaten	P/L	Run To Form %	Impact Value	Market Value
Richard Hannon	56	532	10.53%	51.25	-153.85	25.95	1.05	1.31
John Gosden	48	198	24.24%	67.61	26.34	48.96	2.33	2.33
William Haggas	40	181	22.10%	64.03	6.33	35.23	2.19	2.22
Brian Meehan	17	187	9.09%	52.47	11.38	26.19	0.97	1.04
Sir Michael Stoute	17	123	13.82%	58.47	-47.21	32.50	1.30	1.93
Andrew Balding	17	173	9.83%	53.22	-10.83	33.42	0.98	1.19
Charles Hills	17	199	8.54%	52.24	-52.13	28.38	0.85	1.08
Ralph Beckett	17	139	12.23%	58.03	-28.21	34.55	1.27	1.44
Roger Charlton	16	120	13.33%	51.50	5.70	27.59	1.41	1.51
Charlie Appleby	14	67	20.90%	63.26	-13.76	36.10	1.73	2.02

NEWCASTLE (AW)

Trainer	Wins	Runs	Strike Rate	% Rivals Beaten	P/L	Run To Form %	Impact Value	Market Value
Richard Fahey	46	379	12.14%	56.00	-47.38	26.42	1.13	1.25
Jim Goldie	29	243	11.93%	54.07	21.33	19.10	1.23	1.14
John Gosden	28	77	36.36%	74.23	-2.51	56.04	2.98	3.06
Michael Easterby	25	186	13.44%	52.47	78.08	21.68	1.42	1.19
Mark Johnston	25	235	10.64%	49.67	-77.52	21.16	0.89	1.32
David O'Meara	21	253	8.30%	54.10	-78.40	18.01	0.84	1.34
Hugo Palmer	20	85	23.53%	57.15	-0.47	33.26	2.16	1.94
Brian Ellison	20	239	8.37%	51.67	-39.59	20.85	0.86	1.24
Kevin Ryan	20	178	11.24%	54.02	-40.19	21.81	1.04	1.38
Michael Dods	19	161	11.80%	49.63	-25.49	24.20	1.17	1.09

TRAINERS FOR COURSES

NEWMARKET (JULY)

Trainer	Wins	Runs	Strike Rate	% Rivals Beaten	P/L	Run To Form %	Impact Value	Market Value
Richard Hannon	55	408	13.48%	54.44	-68.40	33.19	1.11	1.19
Mark Johnston	45	228	19.74%	52.00	4.60	32.02	1.51	1.39
Charlie Appleby	43	211	20.38%	61.38	-33.72	41.43	1.72	2.01
John Gosden	38	220	17.27%	55.23	-7.60	31.08	1.44	1.90
Saeed bin Suroor	24	105	22.86%	64.98	4.12	37.46	1.87	1.95
William Haggas	23	145	15.86%	53.27	-40.60	28.26	1.31	1.58
Richard Fahey	20	161	12.42%	56.56	11.50	25.71	1.14	1.14
Charles Hills	19	159	11.95%	49.01	-48.04	25.87	1.01	1.27
Sir Michael Stoute	17	137	12.41%	51.59	-77.46	24.81	1.08	1.61
Ralph Beckett	17	97	17.53%	54.73	-8.38	33.51	1.37	1.33

NEWMARKET (ROWLEY)

Trainer	Wins	Runs	Strike Rate	% Rivals Beaten	P/L	Run To Form %	Impact Value	Market Value
John Gosden	63	326	19.33%	61.37	-1.71	41.04	1.83	1.90
Charlie Appleby	52	207	25.12%	61.37	50.91	37.90	2.27	1.90
Richard Hannon	41	350	11.71%	52.69	47.20	32.71	1.10	1.16
Aidan O'Brien, Ireland	31	142	21.83%	65.19	23.64	47.89	2.05	2.17
Mark Johnston	27	250	10.80%	50.94	-46.75	30.94	1.02	1.09
Saeed bin Suroor	27	146	18.49%	62.37	1.63	35.78	1.78	1.85
Roger Varian	22	201	10.95%	53.73	-41.50	33.61	1.13	1.40
William Haggas	20	196	10.20%	53.07	-37.80	22.63	1.05	1.62
Sir Michael Stoute	18	171	10.53%	51.69	-64.63	28.56	1.03	1.56
Ralph Beckett	15	119	12.61%	53.64	-19.22	34.52	1.28	1.36

NOTTINGHAM

Trainer	Wins	Runs	Strike Rate	% Rivals Beaten	P/L	Run To Form %	Impact Value	Market Value
Richard Fahey	38	221	17.19%	56.41	37.01	26.09	1.48	1.32
Michael Appleby	38	261	14.56%	48.65	13.20	21.22	1.33	1.16
Richard Hannon	26	177	14.69%	57.65	-39.66	30.23	1.30	1.47
John Gosden	23	130	17.69%	63.97	-7.70	41.19	1.70	2.38
Roger Varian	19	108	17.59%	59.91	-27.12	45.87	1.66	1.83
Mark Johnston	19	143	13.29%	52.24	-61.35	27.86	1.02	1.37
Clive Cox	19	99	19.19%	60.73	-2.55	39.92	1.79	1.53
Mick Channon	19	136	13.97%	55.21	47.40	30.32	1.27	1.26
Sir Michael Stoute	17	87	19.54%	59.65	-0.54	48.85	1.74	1.80
K. R. Burke	16	98	16.33%	59.10	22.75	33.88	1.42	1.21

PONTEFRACT

Trainer	Wins	Runs	Strike Rate	% Rivals Beaten	P/L	Run To Form %	Impact Value	Market Value
Richard Fahey	55	314	17.52%	58.51	42.38	26.85	1.42	1.37
Mark Johnston	34	197	17.26%	50.92	-71.05	30.64	1.26	1.49
Tim Easterby	25	197	12.69%	50.62	-28.67	21.39	1.12	1.02
David O'Meara	18	163	11.04%	52.33	-53.50	16.98	0.95	1.22
Kevin Ryan	16	109	14.68%	52.73	16.71	26.89	1.24	1.14
Micky Hammond	15	154	9.74%	44.57	-41.75	19.93	0.85	0.83
Sir Michael Stoute	13	56	23.21%	63.71	-17.06	47.29	1.58	1.94
Michael Appleby	13	105	12.38%	48.45	-33.83	19.05	1.08	1.08
Richard Whitaker	12	60	20.00%	59.59	13.08	25.00	1.87	1.10
Mick Channon	12	58	20.69%	62.13	41.50	34.48	1.81	1.45

REDCAR

Trainer	Wins	Runs	Strike Rate	% Rivals Beaten	P/L	Run To Form %	Impact Value	Market Value
Richard Fahey	51	322	15.84%	60.83	-9.85	31.23	1.67	1.63
David O'Meara	38	251	15.14%	57.26	-19.61	25.21	1.51	1.51
Tim Easterby	33	432	7.64%	51.01	-165.44	19.59	0.86	1.04
Michael Dods	25	211	11.85%	52.37	-18.09	25.68	1.30	1.34
Kevin Ryan	23	161	14.29%	59.24	-54.15	28.22	1.53	1.62
Mark Johnston	20	126	15.87%	52.13	-12.50	24.19	1.47	1.40
Michael Easterby	14	149	9.40%	46.05	-52.13	14.88	1.03	0.96
William Haggas	14	35	40.00%	72.63	5.55	48.57	3.57	3.12
David Barron	14	102	13.73%	58.09	42.13	30.24	1.55	1.37
Ruth Carr	14	170	8.24%	54.04	-74.50	15.51	0.95	1.26

RIPON

Trainer	Wins	Runs	Strike Rate	% Rivals Beaten	P/L	Run To Form %	Impact Value	Market Value
David O'Meara	46	291	15.81%	53.71	4.19	24.00	1.32	1.35
Tim Easterby	44	419	10.50%	51.22	-94.13	21.72	0.92	1.08
Richard Fahey	43	339	12.68%	54.21	-96.84	25.41	1.10	1.42
Mark Johnston	33	211	15.64%	51.45	0.87	28.17	1.11	1.33
William Haggas	22	49	44.90%	72.57	11.18	58.61	3.28	2.95
Ruth Carr	13	111	11.71%	54.84	45.25	18.92	1.14	1.16
David Barron	11	114	9.65%	50.14	-40.40	16.75	0.90	1.24
Richard Whitaker	11	77	14.29%	51.97	27.25	23.38	1.42	0.95
Ann Duffield	10	83	12.05%	51.62	-15.21	27.15	0.99	0.95
John Quinn	10	73	13.70%	52.87	7.60	24.66	1.24	1.22

SALISBURY

Trainer	Wins	Runs	Strike Rate	% Rivals Beaten	P/L	Run To Form %	Impact Value	Market Value
Richard Hannon	58	409	14.18%	55.90	-56.21	31.73	1.14	1.56
Andrew Balding	30	172	17.44%	54.10	-15.46	34.37	1.50	1.50
Ralph Beckett	25	152	16.45%	58.60	-19.96	35.05	1.40	1.53
Clive Cox	17	116	14.66%	51.70	-35.90	29.51	1.28	1.38
Rod Millman	16	153	10.46%	49.07	-40.58	19.04	0.90	1.00
Mick Channon	14	158	8.86%	50.89	-55.07	23.87	0.72	1.05
Charles Hills	13	92	14.13%	56.19	-10.40	28.55	1.22	1.40
Roger Charlton	13	74	17.57%	55.15	-26.98	36.16	1.50	1.63
John Gosden	13	44	29.55%	76.83	37.69	66.57	2.39	2.25
Roger Varian	12	65	18.46%	65.74	2.06	48.35	1.58	1.94

SANDOWN PARK

Trainer	Wins	Runs	Strike Rate	% Rivals Beaten	P/L	Run To Form %	Impact Value	Market Value
Richard Hannon	41	298	13.76%	53.85	-23.87	33.33	1.16	1.20
John Gosden	35	154	22.73%	63.44	0.58	41.27	1.80	1.93
Sir Michael Stoute	33	130	25.38%	63.48	16.42	40.33	2.08	1.88
Clive Cox	20	109	18.35%	54.01	22.71	36.20	1.53	1.34
William Haggas	17	69	24.64%	63.41	7.01	41.16	1.98	2.02
Roger Varian	16	79	20.25%	61.67	-18.63	39.61	1.75	1.81
Andrew Balding	16	162	9.88%	53.67	-29.48	32.19	0.81	1.19
Roger Charlton	13	66	19.70%	54.41	-17.27	37.94	1.65	1.70
Charlie Appleby	13	75	17.33%	59.99	-15.27	42.42	1.31	1.79
Mark Johnston	13	115	11.30%	44.03	-61.54	25.81	0.91	1.26

SOUTHWELL (AW)

Trainer	Wins	Runs	Strike Rate	% Rivals Beaten	P/L	Run To Form %	Impact Value	Market Value
Michael Appleby	117	753	15.54%	56.56	-189.89	21.96	1.24	1.50
Scott Dixon	53	568	9.33%	49.67	-8.10	16.63	0.85	1.00
Richard Fahey	35	198	17.68%	57.27	-32.99	27.27	1.41	1.38
Derek Shaw	35	261	13.41%	51.65	33.88	20.94	1.18	1.06
K. R. Burke	32	144	22.22%	58.04	132.66	33.44	1.63	1.28
David Evans	31	219	14.16%	54.87	10.04	25.02	1.09	1.21
Andrew Balding	28	100	28.00%	68.81	-1.47	39.48	2.01	2.03
Roy Bowring	25	181	13.81%	53.57	-17.60	19.68	1.23	1.17
Mark Johnston	24	134	17.91%	56.00	-24.54	26.81	1.23	1.61
Keith Dalgleish	24	162	14.81%	50.73	-9.08	25.44	1.19	1.42

THIRSK

Trainer	Wins	Runs	Strike Rate	% Rivals Beaten	P/L	Run To Form %	Impact Value	Market Value
Richard Fahey	50	301	16.61%	61.97	14.17	32.66	1.57	1.53
David O'Meara	31	241	12.86%	57.42	-30.47	23.08	1.29	1.53
Tim Easterby	29	370	7.84%	47.06	-95.88	18.34	0.77	1.01
Michael Dods	26	233	11.16%	54.10	-42.38	21.85	1.17	1.36
Kevin Ryan	23	202	11.39%	47.57	-51.71	20.35	1.13	1.31
Paul Midgley	14	100	14.00%	53.56	9.25	17.39	1.50	1.13
Ruth Carr	14	202	6.93%	50.21	-68.30	12.44	0.80	1.12
Keith Dalgleish	14	66	21.21%	59.72	46.21	28.06	2.22	1.39
Brian Ellison	12	109	11.01%	44.71	1.88	23.14	0.99	0.86
Bryan Smart	11	72	15.28%	56.87	14.38	22.64	1.50	1.14

WETHERBY

Trainer	Wins	Runs	Strike Rate	% Rivals Beaten	P/L	Run To Form %	Impact Value	Market Value
Richard Fahey	6	29	20.69%	63.41	16.25	33.62	1.94	1.63
Tim Easterby	5	34	14.71%	59.61	9.80	30.72	1.48	1.05
David O'Meara	5	28	17.86%	67.33	45.75	28.57	2.05	1.85
Mark Johnston	3	15	20.00%	55.40	10.10	28.00	1.59	1.77
Ruth Carr	3	22	13.64%	46.35	-3.00	14.29	1.49	1.17
Declan Carroll	3	11	27.27%	50.97	11.00	27.27	2.78	1.32
Kevin Ryan	3	19	15.79%	48.97	24.50	15.79	1.64	1.18
John Gosden	3	4	75.00%	86.54	8.00	75.00	8.46	3.10
David Brown	2	2	100.00%	100.00	26.00	100.00	11.67	0.87
Antony Brittain	2	10	20.00%	56.96	5.50	20.00	2.17	1.13

WINDSOR

Trainer	Wins	Runs	Strike Rate	% Rivals Beaten	P/L	Run To Form %	Impact Value	Market Value
Richard Hannon	64	409	15.65%	55.71	-98.83	29.74	1.33	1.62
Clive Cox	40	187	21.39%	62.69	26.47	35.91	1.88	1.70
Roger Varian	31	100	31.00%	65.26	25.17	44.88	2.73	2.33
Ralph Beckett	26	128	20.31%	59.88	-9.54	40.09	1.76	1.82
David Evans	24	241	9.96%	49.23	-106.08	16.61	0.86	1.04
Henry Candy	22	122	18.03%	59.70	7.75	40.05	1.64	1.54
Ed Walker	22	103	21.36%	66.27	-7.75	43.74	1.94	1.44
Andrew Balding	21	150	14.00%	61.46	-55.10	38.78	1.22	1.58
Charles Hills	20	146	13.70%	53.66	-5.75	22.86	1.25	1.32
Roger Charlton	20	103	19.42%	61.38	-8.81	37.11	1.76	1.96

TRAINERS FOR COURSES

WOLVERHAMPTON (AW)

Trainer	Wins	Runs	Strike Rate	% Rivals Beaten	P/L	Run To Form %	Impact Value	Market Value
Mark Johnston	81	491	16.50%	56.80	-107.75	29.42	1.28	1.43
Richard Fahey	74	598	12.37%	53.05	-82.61	21.54	1.06	1.22
David Evans	74	706	10.48%	50.75	-197.70	19.29	0.91	1.16
Michael Appleby	70	603	11.61%	51.70	-145.53	20.54	1.02	1.20
John Gosden	61	187	32.62%	72.15	-0.81	53.32	2.73	2.70
Daniel Loughnane	60	669	8.97%	50.57	-194.40	16.66	0.84	1.08
Tom Dascombe	60	433	13.86%	56.26	33.02	27.57	1.17	1.41
Charlie Appleby	57	173	32.95%	70.90	-24.12	46.28	2.56	2.64
Tony Carroll	56	528	10.61%	49.33	-119.72	18.86	0.97	1.05
Jamie Osborne	52	363	14.33%	54.20	-112.68	24.94	1.21	1.35

YARMOUTH

Trainer	Wins	Runs	Strike Rate	% Rivals Beaten	P/L	Run To Form %	Impact Value	Market Value
William Haggas	34	131	25.95%	64.90	-1.80	41.29	2.04	2.14
David Simcock	27	100	27.00%	58.06	57.38	39.55	1.85	1.28
Roger Varian	24	98	24.49%	71.93	0.73	53.20	1.96	1.82
John Gosden	23	73	31.51%	72.10	21.69	53.48	2.67	2.18
Stuart Williams	18	99	18.18%	58.50	-0.38	33.74	1.34	1.15
Chris Wall	18	93	19.35%	51.26	-19.81	30.70	1.61	1.43
Chris Dwyer	17	108	15.74%	53.36	29.13	25.43	1.21	1.01
Michael Bell	16	98	16.33%	52.76	1.91	35.56	1.27	1.08
Mark Johnston	15	75	20.00%	50.26	59.22	31.29	1.31	1.10
Sir Michael Stoute	13	66	19.70%	58.23	-22.49	41.05	1.53	1.75

YORK

Trainer	Wins	Runs	Strike Rate	% Rivals Beaten	P/L	Run To Form %	Impact Value	Market Value
Richard Fahey	44	646	6.81%	51.49	-191.50	18.21	0.78	1.17
William Haggas	34	187	18.18%	60.90	3.55	33.34	2.02	1.96
David O'Meara	31	423	7.33%	48.60	-134.75	13.86	0.95	1.27
Mark Johnston	27	265	10.19%	47.97	-17.64	19.83	1.16	1.27
Tim Easterby	26	360	7.22%	50.60	-86.50	17.84	0.93	1.12
Kevin Ryan	25	284	8.80%	53.18	-93.15	22.41	1.06	1.31
Sir Michael Stoute	21	104	20.19%	64.07	1.17	29.81	1.96	2.00
John Gosden	21	86	24.42%	59.75	-0.35	41.20	2.18	2.08
Michael Dods	15	99	15.15%	61.19	24.17	26.51	1.95	1.44
Charlie Appleby	15	73	20.55%	55.04	1.30	32.88	2.29	1.79

INDEX